Exotic Mexican Cuisine

Prabhjot Mundhir

UNICORN BOOKS

Publisher

UNICORN BOOKS

F-2/16, Ansari Road, Daryaganj, New Delhi-110002

☎ 011-23275434, 23262683, 23250704 • *Fax:* 011-23257790

E-mail: info@unicornbooks.in • *Website:* www.unicornbooks.in

Branch : Mumbai

23-25, Zaoba Wadi Thakurdwar, Mumbai-401002

☎ 022-22010941, 022-22053387

E-mail: rapidex@bom5.vsnl.net.in

Showroom :

★ **PM Publications,** New Delhi
- 10-B, Netaji Subhash Marg, Daryaganj New Delhi-110002
- 6686, Khari Baoli, Delhi-110006

Distributors :

★ **Pustak Mahal,** New Delhi

Delhi: ☎ 011-23276539

Bengaluru: ☎ 080-22234025

Patna: ☎ 0612-3294193

★ **V & S Publishers,** Hyderabad

☎ 040-24737290

ISBN 978-81-7806-302-7

Exotic Mexican Cuisine

Edition: 2012

Printed at : *Unique Color Carton, Mayapuri, New Delhi-110064*

Contents

Desserts **131**

Raspberry Sorbet

Preface

Mexican cuisine is very close to my heart. I was introduced to it in the early eighties by my brother, who was a chef and then freshly out of the catering college. We were transferred to Delhi and he happened to be there during winters. My husband had picked up his next rank and a celebration was due for the family and friends. My brother (late Pavender Singh Kalsi) suggested to have Mexican menu/layout. After a little discussion, the idea appealed to us, and we all had a grand theme party. Food was appreciated by one and all. Since the Mexican cuisine is very near to the Indian cuisine in many ways (though the method of cooking is different in many ways), family developed a liking for it, and I started cooking a few favourites. Often, I cooked Mexican food for the friends and relatives visiting us from the USA and Canada, and they appreciated the authenticity of taste and presentation. I started collecting the recipes from different sources. But, in the year 2008, I happened to be in the USA for a couple of months and was mainly based in New York as my sister was doing a public project and almost daily, our lunch used to be out. Experimenting with a variety of foods, we found the Mexican meals more satisfying and lighter, tastier and sumptuous. That was the time that I started tasting variety and relishing it more. The friends and relatives also started treating me in the best of the restaurants known for Mexican food. The variety enjoyed there inspired me for more research on it. And the result is this book. While developing it, I kept the Indian users in mind, so that they can utilize the book to the maximum and enjoy cooking the Mexican dishes in the Indian kitchens. A few ingredients like certain variety of fresh and dried chillies, the herb epazote and tomatillo used in certain preparations are not available in the Indian stores, but the substitutes are recommended. Though most of the essentials are photographed, yet some of the similar looking salsas are not shot. I hope the readers or the users of the book can understand it. I have also tried to give utilization of some of the leftover food to create the fresh dishes for further use. The special sauces created for the innovative and traditional dishes can be enjoyed by the vegetarian gourmets too.

Enjoy cooking and eating exotic Mexican dishes with friends and relatives!

Foreword

It gives me immense pleasure to associate myself with this book of high calibre and absolute honesty. I know Prabhjot Mundhir for close to a decade and I can tell you that not only is she an avid cook but a great teacher as well, who gets great pleasure in penning down her research and making the home cook's life so much easier. This book shows us that there is more to Mexican food than just nachos, burritos and quesadillas. The recipes are varied and well researched, like the *adobo chicken marinated in pumpkin seeds or the prawns in red sauce or even the courgette Mexicana.* They would provide the reader great dexterity in planning meals and feasts all the year round. In fact, it is a celebration of food and life.

Mexican cuisine is very dear to me. It was one of the first foods I cooked: the vibrancy, the colours and the spices bowled me over. It was like 'art on the plate' and I am happy to say these are perfectly reflected in this book. The recipes provide the exacting insights and know how to equip the cook to chefdom.

Like Indian cuisine, the cuisine of Mexico has great depth and a rich cultural history. There are some other common elements in both, like the use of chillies and paprika, the seamless blend of protein and fibre, the colours and the variety of textures.

Happy cooking!

Dev Malik
Head Chef, Auckland,
New Zealand.

Acknowledgement

I would like to dedicate this book to my sister Navjot Altaf, and thank my family and friends who inspired me to develop this book.

I am also thankful to my husband Wg.Cdr. Mandhir Singh for his unrelenting support. He is not only my inspiration but also an excellent critic whose comments encourage me to achieve nothing else but sheer excellence.

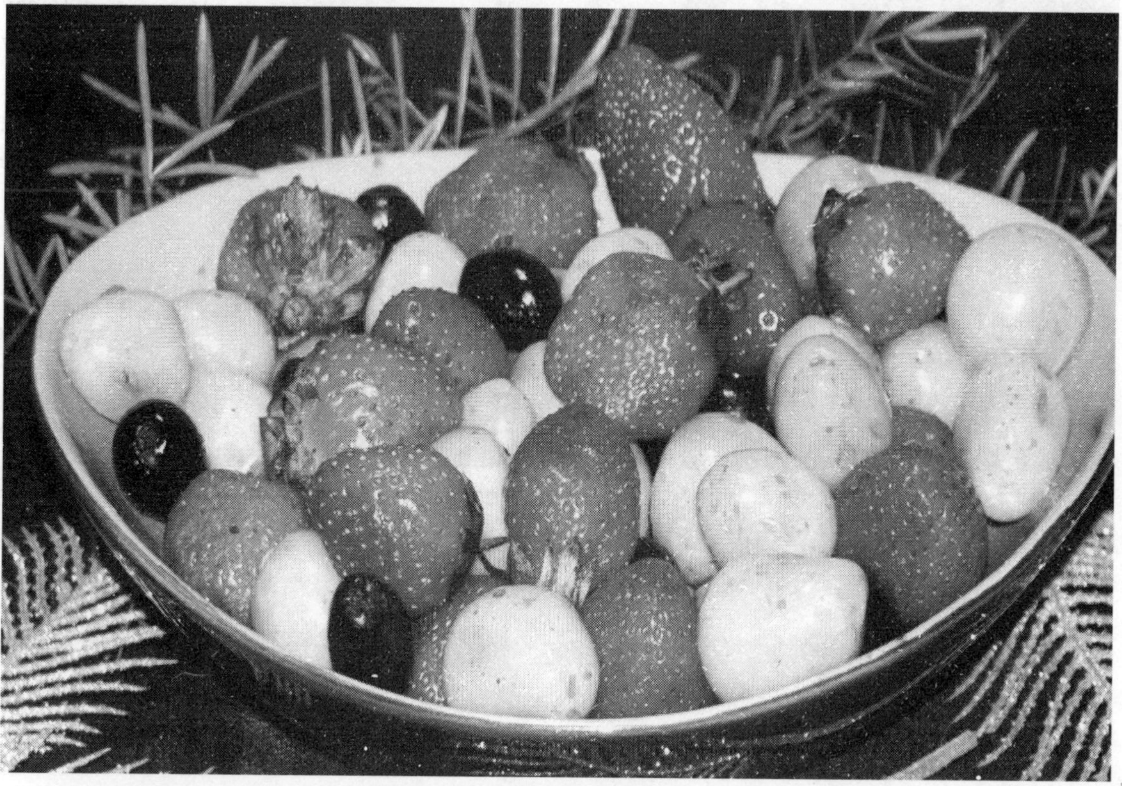

Roasted Berries

Pickled Chillies

Introduction

Mexican food is considered one of the most varied in the world – hot, spicy and colourful. Most of today's Mexican cuisine is based on pre-Hispanic traditions including the Aztec and Maya, combined with the culinary trends introduced by the Spanish colonists. Exotic flavourful recipes produce exciting cuisine and piquancy to the dishes, which is brought by the extensive and careful use of variety of chillies.

From the health point of view, surprisingly, Mexican food is very healthy and it is a vegetarian-friendly cuisine:

- Mexicans use little butter, very little cream and no flour-based sauces. Almost all the sauces are based on thickened vegetable purees. Since most of the sauces are vegetable based, to achieve the wonderful velvety consistency in the sauces, thickening agents such as butter mixed with flour, egg yolks and reduced stocks common in other cuisines are not used. Many of the sauces are made of tomatoes, chillies, garlic and fresh herbs. Thick moles are made of healthful nuts and seeds, such as almonds, walnuts, pine-nuts, peanuts, pumpkin, melon and sesame seeds, etc.
- The dried beans (of course, cooked) served with almost every meal, are excellent source of fiber and minerals.
- Because of the high vegetable contents, all salsas, cooked or raw, contain huge punch of vitamins and minerals. In many forms, salsa, cooked or raw, has been regarded as the healthiest snack in the American super markets only if it is eaten more with healthy fresh corn tortillas and the consumption of chips is restricted. A variety of salsas served with non-vegetarian food too balance the meals.
- Many of the vegetarian savoury preparations can be substituted for the meats, poultry and fish fillings for enchiladas, tacos, la casa dias, wraps and burritos, etc. Mushrooms, corn, beans and other vegetables along with cheese are the best source of getting nutrients for the growth and maintenance of the body.
- The chillies, spices and fresh/dried herbs are carefully and sparingly used to enhance the flavour of food. The use of roasted, skinned and deseeded chillies in food makes it easily digestible.
- Tomatoes and garlic too are roasted, skinned and then chopped for salads, salsas and even for sauces. Occasionally, onions are also roasted on hot grill for use. Skinned tomatoes yield smooth gravies.

- Moreover, a large number of soothing drinks and thirst quenchers are fruit-based.
- Delicious desserts are fruits, nuts and cocoa-based dishes.
- In Mexican cuisine, corn is the main grain and cornmeal is used for cooking delicious pancakes' bread called Tortillas (tor-tee-yah's) which accompany every meal. Since the time immemorial, this bread is an important part of the Mexican diet. Since tortillas are a base for many snacks and main-meal dishes, Mexicans cook tortillas. Historically, tortillas were made exclusively with cornmeal; but unfortunately, these days, commercially, tortillas are made of flour; they are not only tasteless but their nutritional value is also zero. Now the health-conscious people have started making wheat tortillas to prepare wraps, burritos and many more dishes. The grains are also grilled, boiled or made into popcorn or cornflakes.
- We all know that from a nutritional point of view, corn is quite rich in lipids and carbohydrates. "Freshly-ground cornmeal, either white or yellow, has 41.7% protein in every edible pound of corn. It is rich in Calcium, Phosphorus, Potassium, Vitamin A and natural unsaturated oil", says Dr Paul C. Bragg, America's health pioneer (staunch believer of Naturopathy). Corn also contains Vitamin B and one of the sources are whole grains or whole grain cereals. Of the other minerals, whole maize contains chlorine, magnesium, molybdenum, silicon, sodium, sulphur, vanadium, zinc and amino acids.
- In short, corn is considered good for the heart, skin and glowing hair. It is good for heart muscles, stimulates brain action, aids digestion, especially of carbohydrates, reduces fatigue, increases stamina, prevents constipation and also premature ageing by increasing mental alertness. It has a mild diuretic effect. It helps to maintain the normal red blood count and improves circulation, and promotes a healthy skin. It also prevents oedema or fluid retention in connection with the heart ailments.

Certain facts: "The Tehuacan Valley caves of Mexico have furnished evidence for the continuous evolution of maize from 6000 BC to 4000 BC from a pre-historic grass to a stage where the plants carried pods two centimetres long, which, thereafter, increased, both in pod size and productivity. The ancestor is now believed to have been a perennial wild grain, teosinte (Zea mexicana) which hybridized with 'diploperennis', another perennial teosinte about 4000 years ago to trigger off an explosive evolution that led to 'zea mays' a cultivated plant. Each of the many forms of corn, sometimes stated to number seven, was associated with an ancient culture, like the Mayan, Aztec, Inca or Chibehan.".

Fish and Corn Cakes

Cooking Methods and Techniques of Mexican Cuisine

Basically there are two cooking methods/techniques that give Mexican food a distinctive taste and flavour. First one is **broiling** (browning, roasting, searing, toasting) on a hot griddle or on open fire/naked flame; and the other one is initial **searing of the pureed sauce ingredients,** that is the 'frying of the sauce'.

Under the first technique, the large green chillies, peppers are first flame-roasted and then peeled; dried chillies are toasted on hot griddle to deepen their flavour and release the aroma. Garlic and sometimes onion also are turned in their skin on a hot, dry surface beside the tomatoes and tomatillos; they blacken and blister while their flavour concentrates and mellows. Meat is seared on open fire. Tortillas are cooked on the dry iron or clay surfaces. That way the flavours intensify, they deepen and take on a savoury earthiness.

With the application of second technique, the pureed sauce ingredients are fried in a little fat in a hot pan vigorously and concentrate into a mass. The searing sets this sauce apart.

Besides this, Mexican cooking includes a lot of grinding on a rock slab (metate). Earlier, even the corn was crushed on a rock slab to make the dough for tortillas. They also grind dehydrated chillies, nuts, seeds and cacao beans etc. on a rock slab. A bowl-shaped rock mortar (molcajete) is used for grinding spices and ingredients for guacamole etc. because it contains the juices of avocado, chilli, tomatoes and tomatillos, etc.

Roasted Peppers and Tomatoes

A Few Words about Mexican Chillies

In Mexico, chillies are available in many different sizes, shapes and colours. They are fresh, dried, smoked and pickled. They provide many flavours; colours and textures; and above all, make the Mexican cuisine unique. Chillies contain an essential oil containing capsaicin (a bitter compound), which gives chillies their hot piquant flavour and is considered to be good for the heart and blood circulation.

The most popular fresh chillies used in Mexican cuisine are **Habanero** – the hottest of all chillies; **Jalapeno** – extensively used in salsas and cooked dishes; **Poblano** – the largest of chillies of dark green colour with pointed tip which is always cooked before use, skin and veins removed and then extensively used in soups, rice, meat and fish dishes; **Serrano** – another popular thin chilli but hot in nature and used in salsas, guacamole and cooked dishes.

Besides fresh chillies, a wide variety of dried chillies are used in Mexican cuisine and each one is known for its own distinctive colour and flavour. They are mostly used with other ingredients to make classic Mexican chilli sauces to flavour dishes. For example, **Adobo,** a seasoning sauce made with ground dried chillies, herbs and vinegar; and **Mole** – a cooked sauce made with dried chillies, spices, seeds, dry fruits, a toasted corn tortilla and sometimes a piece of chocolate.

Ancho is a dried poblano with a dark wrinkled skin.

Arbol is a very hot dried chilli with lovely red colour and is mainly used in sauces and casseroles.

Chipotle is dried jalapeno which has been dried with warm smoke.

Guajillo is an elegant burgundy-red colour dried chilli and the sauce made with it is medium hot and has a rich colour.

Pasilla is a long and narrow dried chilli with dark brown colour. Its flavour varies from medium-hot to very hot. It is used in mole sauces.

Note: If you want to have a **mildly flavoured** dish, add the whole chilli during cooking and discard it before serving.

For a **slightly hot piquant flavour,** cut the chillies in half lengthwise and remove the veins and seeds before using it in the dish.

For a **strong, hot, full flavour**, chop the chilli flesh along with seeds and veins and add to the dish.

Eating the Mexican Way

The Breakfast (desayuno): The working day in Mexico either starts very early in the morning with a light breakfast of coffee and a sweet roll, or slightly later with a full blown desayuno. The wholesome and nutritional breakfast starts with a plate of fresh seasonal fruit and a glass of fruit juice, oranges, strawberries, limes, mangoes and papayas, etc. are served in a variety.

Next come the eggs in a row, cooked in different ways and accompanied by beans, sauces and tortillas/crusty bread.

The most popular preparations are scrambled eggs, green beans omelette, poached and fried eggs on tortillas with ranchero sauce.

Sweet rolls, coffee and hot chocolate rounds off the breakfast perfectly.

Lunch (la comida): The main meal of the day mostly starts after two o'clock. The opening course starts with a soup followed by a plate of rice. Next main dish of meat or fish is served accompanied by vegetables, salads and beans etc. Chilli sauce and warm tortillas are on offer throughout the meal. The lunch is rounded off with seasonal fruit or dessert. Fresh fruit juices (**agues frescas**) are offered during the meal. Such thirst quenchers are enjoyed at any time of the day.

Supper (la cena): "Supper tends to be a light meal and is mostly served between eight and nine o'clock. Sometimes, a snack is prepared or some of the lunch items are reheated. In summer, a crisp salad or fresh fruit medley is sufficient," say the authors of Fresh Mexican.

Special snacks: On special occasions or on weekends, appetizers (botanas) are served before the main meal, generally accompanied by a drink. Antojitos are also served in between the two main meals to satiate the hunger. They are either prepared or bought from the vendors. A variety ranges from tacos, quesadillas, tostadas, to fresh cheese and guacamole with chips etc. In nutshell, whatever the time of the day, one can find something or the other to satisfy the timely/untimely hunger in Mexico.

Corn Tortillas

Essential Equipment

Most of the cooking utensils and most of the equipment, that were used in Mexico before the arrival of Spanish, are still used for preparing traditional Mexican dishes. The grinding stone and grinding pin (**metate and mano**), mortar and pestle (**molcajete and mano**), the earthenware griddle (**comal**), wooden chocolate whisk (**molinillo**) and wooden tortilla press (**prensa para tortilla**) can still be seen in the rural areas in the central part of the country. In fact, the most sophisticated meals can be made with the simplest equipment. With the development of new electrical gadgets, many time-saving devices are used presently. For example, mixers/food processors are used for grinding and blending; heavy-based iron pans are being replaced by non-stick pans and pots and metal knives are used in place of iron knives.

The following equipment is recommended in modern kitchens:

Blender/food processor, fine mesh sieves, heavy-based small and large sauce pans, iron griddle (like tava), tortilla press (like poori maker), kitchen tongs, kitchen knives and an oven.

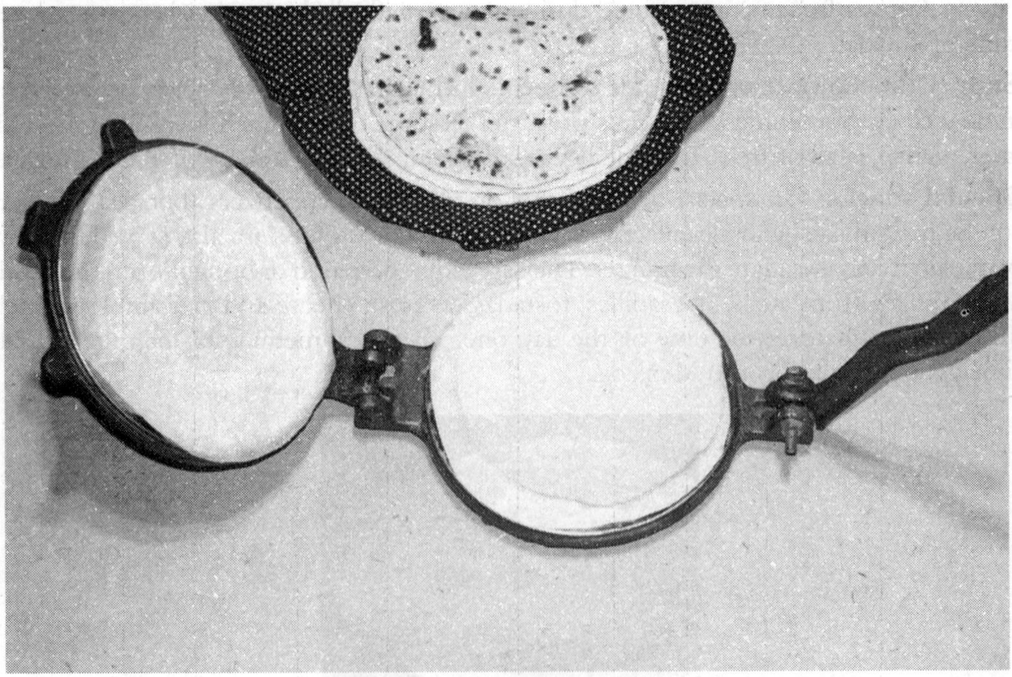

Tortilla Press

Mexican Ingredients

Mexican ingredients are no different than the cooking ingredients used all over the world to create various dishes. It is only the use of selected ingredients in certain quantities that balances food and sets any cuisine apart – and Mexican cuisine is no exemption. The important ones are enlisted here.

Avocados (aguacates): These are widely used all over Mexico in sauces, soups, salads, snacks and main dishes. It is advised to prepare them just before serving or preparing guacamole because their flesh start turning brown soon after they are cut. Sprinkling them with lime juice helps to keep the cut pieces green.

If after making guacamole, the stone of avocado is placed in the sauce before refrigerating it, that too avoids discolouration of the sauce. Stone should be removed before serving the sauce.

Note: In India, avocado is known as **Ramphal.** Avocadoes should be bought a couple of days in advance, as the absolutely ripe ones are rarely sold. Once they are ripe, they can be stored under refrigeration for 3 to 4 days

Beans (frijoles) are one of the staple foods of Mexico. Rich in protein and fibre, they are used extensively along with chillies and maize. They are used in many snacks, soups, side dishes and main dishes. Different kinds of beans, varying in colour and size are used in the Mexican cuisine. Dry beans – such as kidney beans, pinto beans, chickpeas and black beans are in extensive use.

Cereals: Mainly fresh and dry corn, flour and rice are used all over.

Cheese (queso) Oaxaca and **Chihuahua**, good melting cheese are mainly used in snacks and main dishes. They can be substituted with **Mozzarella** and mild **Cheddar cheese. Queso fresco**, a fresh cheese is eaten by itself as an appetizer (botana); this slightly salty cheese is also crumbled over antojitos, salads, soups and main dishes. **Greek Feta cheese** is a good substitute for it. **Queso panela** – a low salt fresh cheese is used in snacks as grilled cheese.

Note: These days in India, a variety of imported cheese are available in selected stores, but otherwise **a range of Amul cheese** can be effectively used for home cooking.

Chillies (chiles): In Mexico, chillies are available in many different sizes, shapes and colours. They are fresh, dried, smoked and pickled. They provide many flavours; colours and textures; and above all, make the Mexican cuisine unique. Chillies contain an essential oil containing capsaicin (a bitter compound), which gives chillies their hot piquant flavour and is considered to be good for the heart and blood circulation.

Fresh chillies (chiles frescos): The most popular used in Mexican cuisine are *Habanero* – the hottest of all chillies; **Jalapeno** – extensively used in salsas and cooked dishes; *Poblano* – the largest of chillies of dark green colour with pointed tip, which is always cooked before use, skin and veins removed and then extensively used in soups, rice, meat and fish dishes; *Serrano* – another popular thin chilli but hot in nature and used in salsas, guccamole and cooked dishes.

Dried chillies (chiles secos): Along with fresh chillies, a wide variety of dried chillies are used in the Mexican cuisine and each one is known for its own distinctive colour and flavour. They are mostly used with other ingredients to make classic Mexican chilli sauces to flavour dishes. For example, *Adobo,* a seasoning sauce made with ground dried chillies, herbs and vinegar; and ***Mole*** – a cooked sauce made with dried chillies, spices, seeds, dry fruits, a toasted corn tortilla and sometimes a piece of chocolate.

Ancho is a dried poblano with a dark wrinkled skin.

Arbol is a very hot dried chilli with lovely red colour and is mainly used in sauces and casseroles.

Chipotle is dried jalapeno which has been dried with warm smoke.

Guajillo is an elegant burgundy-red colour dried chilli and the sauce made with it is medium hot and has a rich colour.

Pasilla is a long and narrow dried chilli with dark brown colour. Its flavour varies from medium-hot to very hot. It is used in mole sauces.

Note: If you want to have a **mildly flavoured** dish, add the whole chilli during cooking and discard it before serving.

For a **slightly hot piquant flavour,** cut the chillies in half lengthwise and remove the veins and seeds before using it in the dish.

For a **strong, hot, full flavour**, chop the chilli flesh along with seeds and veins and add to the dish.

Chocolate: It is made from the seeds of the cacao tree. Cacao beans are ground with sugar and formed into tablets in Mexico. Frequently, cinnamon, almonds and vanilla are added. This type of chocolate is used to prepare drinks and, in small quantity, is added to mole sauces.

Cinnamon (canela): It is used in both savoury and sweet dishes. Mexican cinnamon disintegrates in the dish when added the whole stick.

Coriander (cilantro): It gives an aromatic flavour to the soups, salads, salsas and main dishes. It is extensively used in Mexican dishes and mostly added chopped just before serving the dishes. This herb is considered rich in vitamin B, folic acid and essential oils.

Epazote: This special, highly aromatic, strong smelling herb is used in Mexico to flavour beans, soups, cooked vegetables and stews. It widely grows all over the country but not available easily except from the Mexican specialty stores. The interesting news is that it has no substitute. Now it can be procured from Mexican specialty stores in dry form.

Fruits and Nuts: Like apples, pineapple, melons, watermelons, mangoes, papayas, raspberries, strawberries, oranges and peaches are either eaten as fruits or used in preparation of juices, ice, ice-creams and smoothies and salads, etc; whereas walnuts, almonds, pine-nuts, pistachio nuts and raisins, etc. are mostly used in salads, desserts and in preparation of various exclusive Mexican sauces. Nuts are mostly toasted for a deeper flavour and then left whole, chopped or ground (as required).

Herbs: Fresh and dry cilantro/coriander, parsley, epazote, oregano, basil and thyme are used. Oregano, parsley and thyme are used dry too.

Limes: Out of limes and lemons, Mexicans use limes for flavouring soups, salads, dips and many other appetizers. They use fresh lime juice for preparing popular lemonade and as one of the ingredients for various other drinks. Even the lime zest is used for flavouring the desserts.

Maize/Corn (maiz): Right from the pre-Hispanic era, maize remains the main staple of the Mexican diet. It is used both fresh and dry. In pre-Hispanic era, it was the main ingredient, not only to feed the body, but also to feed the soul. Native Mexicans used to offer their gods the products made of it. Dried maze is used to obtain 'masa', the dough from which corn tortillas and other masa-based snacks like tacos, enchiladas, flautas and corn chips, etc. are made. Fresh sweet corn is eaten whole as corn-on-the-cob, either boiled or roasted, seasoned with lime, salt and chilli powder. Fresh sweet corn kernels are used in soups, vegetable dishes, sweet and savoury cakes and breads. Fresh sweet corn cobs are often cut and added to casseroles. Even the husks are used to wrap food for steaming or baking.

Meats: Various kinds of meats, poultry and a variety of seafood are part of the Mexican cuisine.

Pumpkin seeds (pepitas): The seeds of various pumpkins are considered a delicacy and eaten either roasted and salted as a snack or used ground as a thickening agent in sauces and savoury dishes. They are used in Mexico much before the Spanish arrival.

Sesame seeds (ajonjoli): Sesame seeds are used toasted to enrich the taste of salads or as a garnish for mole sauces and salads. Their sweet and nutty flavour turns an ordinary dish into extra ordinary one.

Spices: Beside cinnamon, dry hibiscus flowers, coriander and cumin seeds, cloves and all spice berries are used to flavour a variety of food. Mostly Mexicans work with whole spices. They always toast them first for a few seconds on a heavy bottomed fry pan and then grind to a powder just before use. This traditional practice not only intensifies their flavour but also imparts the aroma to the preparations.

Tomato (jitomate): The tomatoes are one of those important essentials which make Mexican cuisine so colourful and exotic. Fresh-n-ripe tomatoes are used in preparation of Mexican dishes since pre-Hispanic times. Roasted, peeled and deseeded tomatoes are cooked in soups, sauces and casseroles. Raw tomatoes are eaten as a part of salad. Tomatoes are one of the main ingredients of famous 'salsa mexicana'.

Tomatillo: It is also called the Mexican green tomatoes, which actually are not tomatoes. This is a tart tasting fruit wrapped in a papery husk (like raspberry). It is used either raw or cooked to prepare the most popular Mexican green sauce such as salsa verde. It is also available canned in Mexican stores.

Vegetables: Other vegetables such as onions, garlic, all kinds of red, green and yellow peppers, carrots, beetroots, brinjals, potatoes, sweetpotatoes, cabbages, courgettes, broccoli and mushrooms, etc. are usually used in various dishes.

1. Cut Avocado, 2. Mango, 3. Avocado, 4. Courgettes, 5. Broccoli, 6. Tomatoes, 7. Chickpeas, 8. Black-beans, 9. Orange, 10. Eggplant, 11. Sweet Peppers, 12. Limes, 13. Corn on Cob, 14. Chillies

Essentials of Mexican Cuisine

Corn Tortillas, 23

Adobo, 35

Sour Cream, 31

Pickled Vegetables, 37

Salsa Mexicana, 28

Peanut Dressing, 40

Guacamole, 32

Pineapple Salsa, 28

Chilli-spiced Croutons, 34

Pico de Gallo, 29

Roasted Garlic-flavoured Blackbean Dip, 32

Roasted Corn Salsa, 30

Roasted Chilli Salsa, 29

Essentials of Mexican Cuisine

Essentials of Mexican cuisine are the basic breads, sauces, dips and dressings around which the whole Mexican cuisine revolves. They are either used as one of the ingredients to prepare the final dishes or the important accompaniments to the finally prepared dishes. Their use in the right way and right quantity, balances the cuisine and makes the Mexican cuisine what it is – healthy, exotic and delectable.

Mexico's Daily Bread

1. Corn Tortillas

(Tortillas de Maiz)

Tortilla is a round, flat and unleavened bread made from corn meal. It is one of the most essentials that forms a base of many Mexican dishes. Tortillas are present in every Mexican meal as bread is in other cultures because corn is the staple diet in Mexico. Plain tortillas are turned into enchiladas, flautas and numerous other dishes. They are always warmed before serving with any meal. Day old tortillas can be transformed into tostadas, tortilla chips and budines.

You Require: **Cooking Time:** 30 minutes

Cornmeal	1 cup	Flour	½ cup
Salt	¼ tsp		

Warm water to knead soft dough

Tortilla press/Indian poori maker

(Tortilla press is no different than our poori maker)

Preparation and Cooking for Basic Tortillas

1. Mix together cornmeal, flour, salt and water together to make it pliable dough.
2. Divide it into 2-inch balls and roll each portion into 6" to 7" thin disc on a floured board or on a four-fold cotton napkin by pressing it with hand dipped in dry cornmeal; rotate the board or napkin and press the ball evenly, so that lifting the tortilla is easier. Cook each tortilla on hot griddle/heavy tawa from both sides.

3. Without applying any oil, Tortilla will puff like a 'phulka'. Place it in a casserole lined with a cotton napkin.

4. Thus, finish rolling and cooking all the tortillas. Pile up and keep them warm.

Or use Indian poori maker press to roll/press tortillas.

1. Cut 2 roundels of a thick plastic; place one on the lower plates of the tortilla press; place 1 ball of the basic dough on that; cover it with the other circle of plastic and press the handle of the tortilla press gently to flatten the dough to a smooth circle.

2. Lift the top of the press and rotate the dough circle, so that the circle is pressed evenly. Rotating the tortilla after the first press, not only makes an evenly thick tortilla, but that tortilla cooks evenly too.

3. Open the press and peel off the top sheet of plastic; gently flip the tortilla on one hand, dough side down, then gently peel off the remaining sheet of the plastic; and cook on hot griddle as instructed above.

Note: While cooking tortillas, heat control is very important. Place the tortilla on medium hot griddle and then increase the heat; as it changes the colour, flip it off and change the side; then press it gently with your finger tips/a napkin or spatula, so that the two layers separate easily and tortilla puffs up. If the heat is not controlled, on low fire, tortilla will become dry and on very high fire, it will start blistering.

Usage: Use basic tortillas for making various Mexican dishes or to serve them with the meals.

Tips: The hot tortillas can be wrapped in foil and kept warm in a very low oven for an hour or so. Cold tortillas can be warmed/reheated over medium heat until just heated through and softened or until toasted and crisp. You may warm them according to the personal preference but they must be warmed just before serving. Warming tortillas before folding or rolling makes them pliable and prevents breaking or cracking.

Information: Tortillas are made from masa, the pliable corn dough that can be used to make all sorts of other dishes. Traditionally, masa used to be obtained from the dried corn kernels, soaked overnight in limed water till the outer skin starts to loosen, then corn was placed in cooking liquids for several hours. When corn was softened, it was rinsed to remove excess lime, then softened corn was drained and ground in communal village mill resulting in soft masa (dough). Nowadays, instant corn masa mix (masa harina) is available which is prepared the same way but then completely dehydrated to a powder, and most Mexicans use that.

2. Basic Flour or Wheat Tortillas

(Tortillas de Harina)

Since commercially, in Mexico and America, flour tortillas are replacing the traditional corn tortillas, which are not only tasteless but also not as healthy as the corn ones. As a result, the health-conscious people have started preferring to have wheat flour tortillas, which are not only lighter and tender but also tastier. As we all know, wheat is any day healthier than the refined flour.

You Require: **Cooking Time:** 15 to 20 minutes to cook basic flour tortillas.

Flour or wheat flour	2 cups	Oil	¼ cup
Salt	1 tsp	Tap water	1/3 to ½ cup

Extra wheat flour to roll the tortillas.

Preparation and Cooking:

1. Combine flour/wheat flour (atta), oil and salt.
2. Knead it with water to pliable dough.
3. Cover and stand it for half an hour.
4. Divide the dough into 8 portions; roll each portion into a thin chapatti with the help of dry flour and cook on hot griddle or non-stick tava from both sides like 'phulkas'.
5. Keep the tortillas wrapped in kitchen napkin or foil (to keep them warm) in a casserole. To keep the tortillas soft, avoid over-cooking.
6. Tortillas can be cooked in advance, sealed in a plastic wrap or foil and stored under refrigeration for a week. Take them out 30 minutes before use.

Usage: Use wheat flour tortillas for making Burritos, Enchiladas and Mexican wraps, etc. or use them with any Mexican meal.

Tips: Combining flour and fat properly is very important for the soft pliable dough to get even-textured tortillas. If you cannot make good dough with hands, you may use the food processor for it.

3. Crisp-fried Tortilla and Chips

(Tostadas or Tostaditas/Totopos)

It is a deep-fried-popular snack made out of day old stale tortillas and served with any of the Mexican salsas.

You Require: **Cooking Time:** 30 minutes.

Corn tortillas	6 to 8 pieces	Salt	to taste
Vegetable oil for deep frying			

Preparation and Cooking:

1. For toastadas, keep the tortillas whole but for chips, cut them into wedges. Cut each tortilla into 6 wedges, cover lightly with a napkin to prevent them from curling and let them dry.
2. Heat oil very hot and then lower the fire, fry each tortilla until light brown and crisp, tossing once in between. Remove from oil, shaking the excess, and place on kitchen oil absorbent paper and sprinkle with salt when still warm.

3. For the chips, put a few tortilla wedges into the oil and stir constantly to keep them separate until light brown and crisp. Drain them on paper towel and season with salt while still warm.

Note: For a party or any other gathering, you can keep them warm and crisp in a very low oven for 30 to 40 minutes.

Tips: At some places, rather than deep frying, tortillas are brushed with oil and simply toasted in the oven to a chewy crispness for the same preparation. For chips, they are cut in wedges after brushing with oil and then toasted. Such preparation of chips is called **'totopos'** (a word used to refer to chips in most parts of Mexico).

4. Salsas/Sauces/Dips and Dressings

Salsa, is a word associated with Mexican food. A bowl of salsa on the table imparts a Mexican flavour even to the simplest meal. A salsa can be made from the raw or cooked ingredients, with or without tomatoes, can be hot or mild in flavour and can vary in the texture. Mostly the ingredients are more or less the same, seasonings differ sometimes according to the preference of the cook and availability of the ingredients. The term 'salsa' originated from the Spanish word for sauce.

a. Red Salsa with Roasted Tomatoes

(Salsa Roja)

Mexican cuisine includes a number of salsas/sauces to prepare certain dishes or to serve with the dishes. And tomato salsa is the most important of all. Here tomatoes are roasted, peeled and then used to make this delicious sauce which is used with tortillas, wraps, and other tortilla-based snacks. It accompanies the corn chips also well.

You Require: **Cooking Time:** 15 minutes.

Ripe tomatoes	500 gm	Cooking oil/olive oil	1 tbsp
Onion chopped	1 medium	Garlic roasted and peeled	1 clove
Fresh chillies, green/red	2 to 3 nos.	Coriander chopped	¼ cup
Vinegar	1 tbsp	Sugar	1 tsp
Salt n pepper	to taste		

Preparation and Cooking:

1. Insert a fork or a tip of the knife in each tomato (stem side), and roast directly over full flame from all sides. Turn by turn, finish roasting all the tomatoes till charred.
2. Cool and peel. Finely chop 2 tomatoes and pass the rest through a blender.
3. Stem, seed and de vein the fresh red or green chillies, and chop them.

4. Heat oil in a pan and sauté chopped onion and green chillies. Add pureed tomatoes and cook for 1 minute. Add chopped tomatoes, salt, pepper and vinegar.
5. Remove from fire and store in a clean glass jar under refrigeration. It can last for a couple of days.

Usage: Use as and when required with any dish or snacks.

Tips: Salsas are an integral part of the Mexican cuisine. You cannot imagine a dish without salsa. Salsas come in many colours. "Their distinctiveness derives from the base ingredients and seasonings. Salsas can be raw or cooked; they can be chopped or pureed".

b. Fresh Green Salsa

(Salsa Verde Cruda)

Traditionally, it is made with 'tomatillos' in Mexico and America where they are available, but here we have used unripe green tomatoes for the recipe. Green tomato salsa is as tasty and refreshing as the red tomato salsa. It makes an excellent accompaniment to tortillas, quesadillas and corn chips.

You Require: **Cooking Time:** 7 minutes.

Green tomatoes	500 gm	Green chillies	2 to 3 nos.
Green pepper	½ no.	Onion	1 nos.
Garlic chopped	1 tbsp	Coriander chopped	¼ cup
Cumin powder	1 tsp levelled	Vinegar	1 tbsp
Oil	1 tbsp	Salt and pepper	to taste
Avocado	1 medium-sized (opt)		

Preparation and Cooking:

1. Wash and chop tomatoes, pepper, green chillies, garlic and onion.
2. Place in an electric blender; add chopped coriander and 1/4 cup water, and blend well.
3. Heat oil in a micro-safe bowl, add tomato mixture and cook for 3 minutes, uncovered on HIGH.
4. Add halved, pitted and peeled avocado, cut into small pieces to the blender and blend at medium speed until smooth; add salt and cumin powder; add cooked tomato mixture and just churn once more for a few seconds. Cool.
5. Cover and store under refrigeration till in use.

Serving: Serve 'Green Salsa' with any Mexican dish. It is very refreshing.

Tips: Tomatillos are not tomatoes, they look very much like unripe tomatoes, but they are covered with a papery husk (as the Raspberries are) and that is removed before use.

Because the heat level of chillies varies, you are advised to begin with making your salsas by using less than recommended chillies in the recipe. If it is still hot and fiery, then add the sweeter element, like more tomatoes, etc.

c. Salsa Mexicana

(Fresh Tomato Chilli Relish)

To be served with any Mexican dish as one of the accompaniments, this salsa retains the freshness of the tomatoes, chillies, onion and garlic (which are the chief ingredients of the Mexican cuisine). Whatever method is applied to prepare this delicious and piquant sauce, is secondary. In every region of Mexico, this relish is available with a texture that ranges from a coarse puree to an assembling of coarsely chopped pieces. It is also known as **'salsa cruda'**.

You Require: **Cooking Time:** 30 minutes.

Onion, finely chopped	1 no. large	Jalapeno finely chopped	1 no.
Garlic cloves finely chopped	6 nos.	Tomatoes roasted	500 gm
Olive oil	¼ cup	Dry oregano	1 tsp
Thyme	¼ tsp (opt)	Sugar	2 tsp
Salt	to taste		

Preparation and Cooking:

1. Heat oil and sauté onion in it till transparent; add jalapeno and garlic; cook for 1 minute and stir in tomatoes, bay leaves, oregano, thyme, salt and sugar.
2. Lower the heat and let the sauce simmer; stir occasionally and cook almost for 15 minutes or till the liquid has evaporated.
3. Cool and store under refrigeration. The sauce can be cooked in advance and stored in a chilled tray; dilute it a bit, adding water whenever warming for use.

Usage: Serve it any time with any Mexican dish.

Variation: Chop onion, chilli, tomatoes and garlic very fine and season with salt and sugar and sprinkle 1 teaspoon lime juice and 1 tbsp water. Mix and stand it for 30 minutes before serving, so that the flavours mingle well. Garnish with fresh chopped coriander and serve.

"The finer the dice, the more the flavours sing in harmony", says the chef Rick Bayless in Authentic Mexican.

d. Pineapple Salsa

It (salsa) should pack a punch and yield a complexity of flavours–hot, sweet, salty and sour, and sometimes with a tilt from acid (usually vinegar or citrus)", says the Chef Roberto Santibanez in his New Mexican table. And pineapple salsa is a perfect example.

You Require: **Preparation Time:** 20 minutes.

Pineapple fresh or preserved	1 cup	Spring onions with their greens	3 nos.
Tomato deseeded	1 no.	Ginger grated	1 tsp
Coriander chopped	¼ cup	Green chillies chopped fine	3 nos.
Lemon juice	3 tbsp	Sugar	1 tsp (opt)
Salt	to taste		

Preparation:

1. Chop pineapple, spring onions and tomato very fine and combine in a serving bowl.
2. Add rest of the ingredients and mix well.
3. Cover with cling film and refrigerate at least for 30 minutes before serving.

Note: If you like, you may put all the ingredients in a blender and grind coarsely.

Serving: Serve this salsa with any Mexican snack.

Tips: If preserved pineapple is being used to prepare this dish, do not add sugar.

e. Pico de Gallo

Like other salsas 'Pico de Gallo' also is one of the indispensables of the Mexican cuisine, and is found on almost, every day, on every Mexican table to accompany tacos, grilled food and enchiladas etc.

You Require: **Preparation Time:** 20 minutes.

Ripe tomatoes	2 nos.	White onion finely chopped	½ cup
Cilantro sprigs chopped fine	½ cup	Jalapeno chopped fine	2 tbsp
Lime juice	from 1 lime	Lemon juice	2 tbsp
Salt	1 tsp or to taste	Olive oil	1 tsp (opt)

Preparation and Cooking:

1. Core the tomatoes and cut them in to half. Squeeze out most of the seeds and cut them into very small dices.
2. Combine and toss the diced tomatoes, onion, cilantro and jalapeno together in a bowl and season it with salt and lime juice. Stir in olive oil; cover and stand it for 15 minutes.

Serving: Serve it with Mexican food.

Tips: This salsa can be made in advance and kept at room temperature for up to 4 hours before serving. Stir and check the seasonings once again before serving.

f. Roasted Chilli Salsa

You Require: **Preparation Time:** 15 minutes

Tomatoes	2 nos.	Jalapeno/hot green chillies	3 to 4 nos.
White onion unpeeled	1 no. small	Garlic unpeeled	2 cloves
Dried oregano	½ tsp	Ground cumin	½ tsp
Black pepper (freshly ground)	to taste	Salt	to taste (opt)

Preparation and Cooking:

1. Place tomatoes, chillies, onion and garlic on hot griddle/pan or comal, and roast until the skins of the vegetables are charred and blistered.

2. Peel onion and garlic; chop them and place in a bowl.
3. Roughly chop tomatoes and chillies and add to the onion-garlic mixture.
4. Season with oregano, cumin and black pepper. Toss to combine.
5. Thin it with water if required.

Serving: Serve it with any Mexican snacks or meals.

g. Roasted Corn Salsa

You Require: **Cooking Time:** 20 minutes.

Sweet corn on the cobs	3 nos.	Red pepper	1 no.
Mild green chillies	3 nos.	Garlic unpeeled	2 cloves
Olive oil	1 tbsp	Cilantro chopped	2 tbsp
Fresh oregano chopped	2 tsp	Dried oregano	½ tsp
Salt	to taste	Lime juice	1 tbsp (opt)

Preparation and Cooking:

1. Brush the corn cobs with oil and roast on direct flame or preheated grill until lightly charred and soft. Remove corn kernels from the cobs with a sharp knife and place in a bowl.
2. Brush red pepper and chillies also with oil and cook on hot griddle with garlic until the skins are charred.
3. Chop red pepper and chillies and squeeze garlic.
4. Add chopped ingredients to the corn; mix chopped coriander and oregano and toss the bowl to combine properly.

   Serving: Serve as an accompaniment.

h. Pumpkin Seed Salsa
(Salsa Pepitas)

Mexicans enjoy pumpkin seeds in variety of ways. They simply roast them and season them with salt for a nutritious and tasty snack; they consume them for making delicious gravies and, along with chillies and tomatoes, convert them into a sauce to be accompanied with various dishes. This simple relish/salsa is one of the examples.

You Require: **Cooking Time:** 15 to 20 minutes.

Fresh green pumpkin seeds	1 cup	Tomatoes	2 nos.
Green chillies chopped	2 nos.	Fresh coriander chopped	2 tbsp
Water	2 to 3 tbsp		

Preparation and Cooking:

1. Roast pumpkin seeds until roasted and golden in colour.
2. Roast tomatoes on a hot griddle until charred and blistered; cool and peel. Chop them roughly.
3. Place roasted pumpkin seeds and water in a blender and process to make a rough paste.
4. Add rest of the ingredients and process again to mix well.

Serving: Serve it as an accompaniment.

i. Sour Cream

A cream dip to be enjoyed with Mexican snacks or to be drizzled on fresh tamales or served with fried tacos, etc. which gives a great pleasure to a foodie.

You Require: **Mixing Time:** 10 minutes for mixing
2 hours for getting hung curd

Hung curd	2 cups	Fresh cream	4 tbsp/¼ cup
Lemon juice	1 tbsp	Salt	½ tsp
White pepper powder	½ tsp		

Preparation:

1. Combine hung curd and cream together in a bowl and mix with a wooden spoon till smooth.
2. Add lemon juice, salt and pepper powder; mix with a light hand. Chill under refrigeration till required.

Serving: Serve it with any Mexican snacks and Corn chips, etc.

It is used for topping snacks too.

Tips: Sour cream can be prepared in advance and stored in the chill tray of your refrigerator for 2 to 3 days without losing its freshness.

To get hung curd, place 3-½ cup freshly set thick curds in a sieve lined with muslin cloth, cover and let the whey drain; remove from the cloth and use as and when required. Or tie the cloth loosely with a string and hang it with tap in the washbasin for 2 hours. Don't forget to collect the whey as it is very healthy mineral water and is full of minerals and vitamins.

How to get homemade thick cream enjoyed by Mexicans?

Pour 1 cup whipping cream into a small saucepan and heat it on low fire until the chill of the cream is just off. Don't let the cream to be very hot. Add 2 tsp buttermilk and place the bowl in a warm place; let the cream culture for 12 to 18 hours, says the writer of Authentic Mexican.

j. Roasted Garlic-flavoured Blackbean Dip

You Require: **Cooking Time:** 35 minutes

Black beans/Urad whole	½ cup	Garlic	3 to 4 cloves
Fresh cream	2 to 3 tbsp	Lemon juice	¼ cup
Green chillies chopped	3 nos.	Pepper powder	½ tsp (opt)
Olive oil	1 and ½ tbsp	Cheese grated for garnishing	1 tbsp
Coriander chopped	1 tbsp (opt)		

Preparation and Cooking:

1. Wash and soak black beans overnight or for 8 hours.
2. Drain and wash beans: place in a pressure cooker and add 2 cups of water. Bring it to a boiling point; close the cooker and place weight. As soon as the pressure builds up, lower the heat and cook it for 20 minutes. Switch off the gas and let the pressure drop itself. Or you may cook beans without a pressure cooker till soft. Add more water, if required.
3. Meantime, roast garlic on hot griddle till its skin turns black; peel and chop it very fine.
4. Strain the beans through a colander (you can use the liquid in a soup).
5. Mash the beans, when still hot, with a wooden spoon till mushy.
6. Mix together beans, garlic, lemon juice, green chillies and cream in a bowl. Stir.
7. Season it with salt and pepper; cover and chill for 30 minutes before use. Sprinkle coriander and mix. Garnish it with grated cheese.

Serving: Serve it with chips or any other fried snacks.

Or spread it on Tortillas for a quick bite.

Use it for making sandwiches with toasted bread slices.

k. Guacamole

(Avocado Dip)

Guacamole is a delicious avocado dip/relish which is used as an accompaniment with corn chips, as a dressing for salads; for preparing exotic chilled and hot soups and even a filling for tortillas. Avocado is known as **Makhanphal** in Hindi. Its buttery yellow-olive pulp when mashed and tasted, spreads over the tongue a comforting texture like custard and hints at a strong herbs like bay, thyme and fennel. The taste of this soothing relish is a bit unique.

You Require: **Preparation Time:** 20 minutes.

Avocado ripe	1 no.	Onion chopped fine	1 small
Coriander chopped	2 tbsp	Green chilli chopped	2 nos.
Tomato	1 (opt)	Lemon juice	1 tbsp
Garlic chopped	2 tsp	Green pepper sauce	a few drops (opt)
Olive oil	1 tbsp (opt)	Salt	to taste

Preparation:

1. Cut avocado in half; remove the stone/pits and scoop out the pulp with a spoon.
2. Mash the pulp with the back of the spoon or long-tined fork till quite pulpy. Add rest of the chopped ingredients and seasonings.
3. Char the skin of the tomato; deseed it and chop very fine. Add to the dip and mix.
4. Chill it properly before serving. It can be served at room temperature also.

Note: It's better to serve it within 1 hour to avoid discolouration. Though lime or lemon juice helps to slow down the darkening, but not much. After making the dip, you return the pits to the prepared guacamole sauce (they retard darkening), pressed directly on the surface to keep out oxidizing; wrap it properly with plastic and refrigerate for a few minutes to let the flavours blend. Remove the pit before serving.

Serving: Serve it with Corn chips/Nachos as an accompaniment.

Use it for spreading on bread while making Cemita/Torta.

Tips: Ripe avocado should be selected for this preparation, otherwise taste of the dip can vary and you have to adjust the seasonings.

l. Guacamole with Tomatillos

(Guacamole de Tomate Verde)

Blended with tomatillos, the avocados make a smooth green sauce, which is just ideal for tacos and other appetizers.

You Require: **Cooking Time:** 30 minutes.

Tomatillos husked and washed	6 nos.	Jalapeno/fresh hot green chillies	2 nos.
Or canned tomatillos, drained		Cilantro chopped	2 tbsp
Onion chopped	½ small	Ripe medium avocado	1 no.
Salt	to taste		

Preparation and Cooking:

1. If using fresh tomatillos, boil them in salted water for 10 minutes or until just soft; drain and place in a blender; otherwise, drain canned tomatillos and place in a blender.
2. Chop and add chillies, onion and cilantro and puree to a coarse mixture.
3. Halve the avocado; scoop the pulp and add it to the tomatillos mixture in the blender; pulse it a few times to combine the two properly. Season it with salt.
4. Scrape the sauce in a bowl; return the pit to the sauce; cover it and let it stand for a few minutes to blend the flavours.

Serving: For the best results, serve it within 2 hours.

m. Refried Beans

(Frijoles Refritos/Pinto Beans)

Pinto beans are one of the various beans used in Mexican cuisine. They are the best accompaniments to tortillas, toastadas and enchiladas. This preparation of beans is also known as 'refried beans'. Here, the term refried does not mean frying again but beans thoroughly mashed while cooking and some cheese incorporated in.

You Require: **Cooking Time:** 45 to 50 minutes if cooked in pressure cooker.

Kidney beans	1 and ½ cup	Garlic chopped	2 tbsp
Onion chopped	1 no.	Chilli powder	1 tsp
Bay leaf	1 no.	Veg. taste-making cube	1 no. (opt)
Ginger powder	½ tsp	Seasonings	to taste
Cheddar cheese	½ cup grated	Cooking oil	2 tbsp
Cilantro chopped	¼ cup	Pineapple chopped	½ cup (opt)
Water/veg. stock	3 to 5 cup		

Preparation and Cooking:

1. Wash and soak pinto beans in plenty of water overnight.
2. Cook with 5 cups of water, chopped onion and garlic, taste-making cube and seasonings till soft, first 10 minutes on high fire and then simmer for 1 to 1½ hours on low fire.

   Or cook in a pressure cooker. Add 3 cups of water and beans in the pressure cooker; bring beans to the boiling point; add rest of the ingredients; place the lid and the weight; cook on high fire till the pressure is built; lower the heat and continue cooking for 40 minutes.
3. Mash the beans with a wooden spoon and stir in grated cheese.
4. Heat oil in a pan and stir the beans in it slowly. Add chopped cilantro and mix once again.

Serving: Serve the beans with Enchiladas/Toastadas/Tacos or with any salad. Garnish with sliced pineapple.

It makes a perfect Mexican meal.

n. Chilli-spiced Croutons

Chilli-spiced croutons add zest and crunch to any green salad and thick and creamy soup. These croutons impart piquant flavour to the food.

You Require: **Cooking Time:** 30 minutes.

White bread slices	10 to 12 nos.	Olive oil	¼ cup
Or bread loaf	1 no.	Chilli powder	1 tbsp heaped
Oregano dried	1 tbsp	Salt	1 tsp

Preparation and Cooking:

1. Preheat an oven.
2. Remove the crust and cut bread loaf or slices into 1-inch pieces.
3. Combine oil, salt, chilli powder and oregano in a large bowl. Tilt the bowl, so that seasoned oil spreads evenly and bowl is well coated with oil.
4. Add bread cubes and toss gently until evenly coated.
5. Spread the croutons on a baking sheet and bake until crisp and golden brown. It may take 15 to 20 minutes.
6. Stir them once during baking to bring those around the edge to the centre or vice-versa.
7. Remove from the oven and let them cool completely. Store them in an air-tight container at room temperature up to 6 to 7 days.

   Serving: Serve them with any Creamy soup or add them to the salads.

o. Adobo

The term 'adobo' stands generally for two concepts. One, for a paste-like product made with chillies, garlic and spices and that is used to marinate meats and poultry; and the second one, of a thinner sauce made with the same ingredients, in which meats and poultry are stewed. Mexicans use dry chillies known as ancho, pasilla, mulato and guajillo, etc. for its preparation. The chillies are wiped clean, seeded, de-veined, then toasted, soaked and ground. The soft chillies are generally blended well to a fine puree with garlic and spices. Sometimes, even a little vinegar is also used to pep up the flavour of the chillies.

You Require: **Preparation Time:** 40 minutes.

Kashmiri chillies whole (broken and deseeded)	1 cup	Onion	1 small
		Garlic peeled	¼ cup
Wine vinegar	½ cup	Salt	2 tsp or to taste
Cumin	1 tsp	Clove powder	1 tsp
Oregano dried	1 tsp	Thyme dried	½ tsp
Vegetable oil	1 tbsp		

Preparation and Cooking:

1. Lightly roast chillies in a hot pan, stirring occasionally and soak them in 2 cups of water for 30 minutes.
2. Strain chillies and save the liquid; place the chillies in a blender along with garlic, cumin, cloves, onion, oregano, thyme salt and vinegar. Blend on medium speed till pureed. Keep adding as much liquid (that is saved) as is required to get the desired result. You may pass it through a sieve.
3. Heat the oil in a pan over medium fire, pour in the chilli mixture and simmer gently for 15 minutes or so.

4. Remove from the fire and transfer into a clean-dry glass jar; place the lid and store under refrigeration. It lasts more for than 15 days under refrigeration and for more than a month in the deep freezer.

Usage: Use this chilli sauce to serve with/for marinating variety of meats/stewing meats and poultry in it or adding to the other sauces to enhance their flavour.

p. Spicy Escabeche/Escabeche Picoso

Escabeche is also known as Ceviche or Seviche. Mexicans make it with cleaned and sliced fish and eat it raw. It is considered a delicacy. But this particular vegetarian preparation can be enjoyed universally by both – veg. and non-vegetarian food lovers.

You Require: **Cooking Time:** 15 minutes.

White onions	2 large	Garlic	3 cloves
Olive oil mild	½ cup	Habanero chilli	1 no.
Jalapeno peppers	4 nos.	Bay leaves	3 nos.
Oregano dried	1 tsp	Thyme dried	½ tsp
Cider vinegar	¼ cup	Salt	to taste

Preparation and Cooking:

1. Clean, peel and cut onions into halves and then into thin slices.
2. Slice garlic cloves too.
3. Chop chillies fine.
4. Heat the oil in a medium-sized pan/skillet over medium fire.
5. Add sliced onions, garlic, chillies, bay leaves, oregano and thyme; cook till onions are translucent but not brown. It may take 8 to 10 minutes for this process.
6. Add salt and vinegar and bring the mixture to a boil; remove the pan from the fire and cool completely.
7. Transfer the mixture into a bowl with a lid and store under refrigeration for upto 2 weeks.

Usage: This preparation of ceviche can be used as a condiment to chicken/fish or as a topping for a filled omelet, or even as a spread on bread or quesadilla before assembling.

Tips: "Habanero is considered as the hottest chilli in the world. It is a small chilli that is shaped like a delicate Japanese lantern, but not delicate in its nature. One chilli with its seeds and ribs intact is enough to cook hot soup or stew. They range in colour from pale green to orange yellow. They are very similar to scotch bonnet chillies, which can be substituted for them and vice-versa," says Roberto Santibanez, chef, Rosa Mexicano, New York.

In that comparison, Jalapeno is a very mild chilli and is commonly used; it is easier to clean and deseed and its flavour improves by roasting. It is mostly found in green colour and sometimes ripens to red.

q. Ranchera Sauce

(Salsa Ranchera)

This is one of the phenomenal tomato based sauces given to the world by Mexicans. This cinnamon and garlic flavoured sauce can not only be spooned over the egg dish cooked for breakfast, but can also be used as a base sauce for other dishes.

You Require: **Cooking Time:** 30 minutes.

Ripe tomatoes	8 large	Onion chopped	2 small
Garlic chopped	2 cloves	Green chillies	4 nos.
Cinnamon stick	1 piece of 2 inches (opt)	Vegetable oil	¼ cup
Salt	to taste	Sugar	1 tsp (if needed)
Parsley chopped	2 tbsp		

Preparation and Cooking:

1. Make the sauce. Roast tomatoes and remove the skin.
2. Chop tomatoes roughly and put them in a blender along with chopped garlic and green chillies and blend to get a smooth texture. You may deseed the chillies for the milder taste.
3. Heat the vegetable oil over a medium heat, add onion and cook till the onions are transparent; add tomato mixture and cinnamon stick; boil for 10 minutes, stirring regularly. Add salt and sugar too. Cook till the sauce has thickened, just enough to coat a spoon.
4. Check the seasoning and keep the sauce warm till required (for immediate use), otherwise, cool and store under refrigeration. The sauce can be cooked up to 3 days in advance.
5. Reheat over medium heat, sprinkle 1 tbsp water if required, to maintain the same consistency. Remove the cinnamon stick.

Usage: Use it to make Rancheros for breakfast or as a base sauce for making Spaghetti or Meatballs, etc.

Tips: Cinnamon is not used traditionally in this dish, but in the central Mexican states, it is not unusual.

If you are using Mexican cinnamon stick, then you should tie it in a piece of cheese/ muslin cloth before adding to the sauce, as Mexican cinnamon falls apart during cooking, so it will be difficult to remove it from the finished dish.

r. Pickled Vegetables

Pickled vegetables are a classic feature of Mexican cuisine and, especially, the pickled chillies. They are a zesty addition to any meal. Mostly jalapeno are combined with other vegetables and offered as a side dish. Pickled jalapenos are also used to top toastadas. Even the pickling liquid (brine) serves as a terrific flavour booster for other dishes. All sorts of vegetables, such as mushrooms, cauliflowers, carrots, onions and beans, etc are used for pickling. In the coastal area of Mexico, fish- and shellfish-pickled dishes are very popular.

You Require: **Cooking Time:** 15 minutes.

Carrots	4 nos.	Cauliflower/broccoli	1 small head
Spring onions	12 nos.	Garlic cloves peeled	4 nos.
Baby potatoes (cooked and peeled)	12 nos.	Button mushrooms	200 gm
Jalapeno			
Or Indian achari mirch	4 to 6 nos.	Olive oil	¼ cup
Cider vinegar	3 cups	Bay leaf	2 nos.
Water	1 cup	Thyme dried	½ tsp
Oregano dried	1 tsp	Peppercorns crushed	1 to 2 tsp
Salt	2 tbsp leveled		

Preparation and Cooking:

1. Clean and cut carrots into sticks; break cauliflower into flowerets: clean and cut the white part of spring onions; scrub and cook baby potatoes and slice chillies into strips.
2. Heat the oil in a large heavy-based pan/kadai and sauté the onion, garlic and carrots over medium fire for 2 minutes; add chillies and cauliflower and cook for 2 minutes; add potatoes and mushrooms and cook for 2 more minutes.
3. In a separate pan, combine vinegar, measured water, salt, herbs and peppercorns and bring the mixture to a boil. Pour over the vegetables and stir.
4. Cool the mixture completely and pour into a glass jar, cover and store under refrigeration. This will last for a long time as far as the vegetables are immersed in brine.

Note: If you want to keep it for a longer period, store it in sterilized bottle, seal it and place in a dark and cool place.

Serving: Serve it with any Mexican meal as a side dish.

Or chop the vegetables and mix with other ingredients prepared for stuffing Enchiladas, Burritos, Pies and Wraps.

Tips: Refrigerate the pickle at least for one day before use.

The pickle lasts even for 1 year under refrigeration, if properly covered with brine solution. Later brine can be used to dilute any sauce.

s. Pickled Chillies

(Chillies en Escabeche)

Mexicans' pickled chillies include a wide variety of chillies in different sizes and colours and are made with home-made fruit vinegar.

You Require: **Cooking Time:** About 30 minutes.

Jalapenos	15 to 20 nos.	Or green Achari mirch	15 to 20 nos.
Vegetable oil	¼ cup	Garlic peeled	6 cloves

Cider vinegar	½ cup	Fruit vinegar	½ cup
Bay leaves	2 nos.	Peppercorns coarsely ground	6 nos.
Salt	½ to 1 tsp	Mixed herbs 1 tsp *(thyme, oregano and marjoram)*	1 tsp

Preparation and Cooking:

1. If you want to use the chillies the same day, seed them and slice, otherwise give a slit on the side of each chilli to allow penetration.
2. Heat oil in a pan over medium fire, add whole garlic cloves and fry until lightly brown; remove from oil and keep aside.
3. Add chillies and stir for 3 minutes.
4. Add ½-cup water, vinegar, fried garlic, bay leaves, herbs, salt and pepper; cover and simmer for 5 to 7 minutes or till chillies are olive green.
5. Remove from fire, pour into a glass jar/non-corrosive container, cool and season with additional salt to taste.
6. Cover and refrigerate for a day before using.

Serving: Serve it with any Mexican meal. Chop and add to the mixture used for Burritos, Tacos, Enchiladas, Pies or Wraps.

Tips: The chillies can last for several months under refrigeration, if the brine solution covers them properly.

t. Pickled Red Onions

(Escabeche de Cebolla)

Delicious sweet-n-sour onions are used for almost every snack. The sandwiches and other vegetarian or non-vegetarian snacks are topped with this richly-spiced onion preparation.

You Require: **Cooking Time:** 15 minutes.

Red onions	2 large	Cumin seeds	¼ tsp
Peppercorns	½ tsp	Dried oregano	½ tsp
Garlic peeled	2 cloves	Salt	½ tsp
White vinegar	½ cup		

Preparation and Cooking;

1. Peel and slice onions to 1/8th-inch thickness; place them in a pan and cover them with salted water. Bring to a boiling point and boil for 1 minute. Remove from the heat and drain. Blanching process removes the harshness of the onions.
2. Coarsely grind the peppercorns and cumin and add to the saucepan along with the remaining ingredients. Pour in enough water to just cover the onions and boil on medium heat for 3 minutes.

3. Remove from the fire and pour into a small glass jar and let them stand for several hours before use.

Usage: Use them to top any snack.

Variation: Take 4 cups sliced red onion; omit cumin, garlic and peppercorns; take half the quantity of vinegar, 1 cup freshly squeezed lime juice and 1 chilli. Toss the onions, salt and oregano well in a bowl. Put them in a tall glass or stainless steel jar; pour vinegar over the onions and then add the lime juice. Lime juice should cover the onions, so, if need be, add some more juice. Cut the tip of the chilli and stick it in the onions. Refrigerate overnight. Bring this to the room temperature before serving.
The preparation can last for a week under refrigeration.

u. Peanut Dressing

This is an excellent dressing to be served with grilled or broiled seafood, steamed beans or asparagus or to toss the green salad with.

You Require: **Preparation Time:** 15 minutes.

Chilli peanuts	1 cup	Lime juice	of 3 nos.
White vinegar	3 tbsp	Orange juice	½ cup
Honey	2 tbsp	Adobo sauce	3 tbsp
Olive oil	1/3 cup		

Preparation:

1. Grind the peanuts in a mixer, using on and off pulses.
2. Pour lime juice, vinegar, orange juice, honey and adobo chilli sauce and whisk.
3. Whisking constantly, drizzle in the olive oil. The honey and chilli sauce help to keep the dressing emulsified.
4. Store the dressing at room temperature up to 3 to 4 hours and under refrigeration for a day. Bring it to room temperature before use.
5. If you feel the dressing is separating before you use it, whisk it again for a while.

v. Roasted Garlic Dressing

It is a simple garlic flavoured, vinegar and oil based dressing that goes very well with mixed fresh greens.

You Require: **Cooking Time:** 15 minutes

Garlic unpeeled	3 cloves large	Balsamic vinegar	3 tbsp
Olive oil	2/3 cup	Black pepper (freshly ground)	¼ tsp
Salt	½ tsp or to taste		

Preparation and Cooking:

1. Roast the garlic on a griddle over medium fire, tossing number of times for 15 minutes or until blackened in spots and soft. Cool and peel off the skin.
2. Combine the garlic and rest of the ingredients in a blender and process until smooth. Check the salt; cover and store at room temperature.

Serving: You may serve it with Jicama cut in matchstick style and tossed with watercress and red onion.

w. Lime-Cilantro Dressing

This creamy dressing, tart in taste, is very tasty, if used on tossed salad of steamed mixed vegetables or tossed salad of mixed lettuce.

You Require: **Preparation Time:** 15 minutes.

Lime zest green 2-inch long and ¼ inch wide strip

Lime juice	40 ml	Garlic peeled	2 cloves small
Fresh green chilli	1 no.	Coriander chopped	2 tbsp
Vegetable oil	2/3 cup	Feta cheese/paneer	2 tbsp (opt)
Salt	to taste		

Preparation:

1. Chop garlic. Seed and chop chilli. Crumble cheese. Put them in a blender.
2. Put the remaining ingredients also in a blender and process until all the ingredients are smooth. Check the salt.
3. Cover and refrigerate.

Usage: Chill and use when required.

x. Jalapeno Dressing

(Adarezo De Jalapeno)

It is a simple and easy-to-make chilli dressing for chicken, vegetables and nuts salad, converts a simple salad of roasted shredded chicken, celery and onions, etc. into an extraordinary dish.

You Require: **Preparation Time:** 15 minutes.

Jalapeno	2 nos.	Dijon mustard	1 tbsp
Lime juice	from 1 lime	White wine vinegar	2 tbsp
Sugar	2 tsp	Salt	2 tsp
Garlic minced	1 clove	Olive oil	¼ cup
Vegetable oil	¼ cup		

Preparation:

1. Combine jalapeno, lime juice, vinegar, sugar, garlic, mustard and salt in a blender and blend at low speed, using on and off pulses, until jalapeno is chopped fine. With the mixer on, add oils in a slow and steady stream.
2. Pour the dressing in a clean glass bottle, cover with a tight lid and refrigerate. The dressing can be prepared one day in advance and refrigerated.
3. Bring it to the room temperature before use. Shake well and use.

Yield: About 1 cup dressing.

Usage: This dressing can also be used with mixed Greens and Avocado salad.

y. Honey-Lime Dressing

(Adarezo De Limony Miel)

It is a sweet, simple and pungent dressing used for shredded chicken combined with fruits and vegetable salad/green salad, is fondly enjoyed in Mexico and many American countries.

You Require: **Preparation Time:** 15 minutes.

Honey	2 tbsp	Fresh lime juice	¼ cup
Wine vinegar	2 tbsp	Mild chilli chopped	1 no.
Garlic chopped	1 clove	Dijon mustard	1 tsp
Salt	2 tsp	Olive oil	¼ cup
Vegetable oil	¼ cup		

Preparation:

1. Combine lime juice, honey, vinegar, chilli, garlic, mustard and salt in a blender and blend at low speed, using on and off pulses, until chilli and garlic are chopped fine. With the mixer on, add oils in a slow and steady stream.
2. Pour the dressing in a clean glass bottle, cover and refrigerate. The dressing can be prepared one day in advance and stored under refrigeration.
3. Bring it to the room temperature before use. Shake well and use.

Usage: Combine it with chicken, fruit or green salad and serve.

Appetizers/Entradas/Botanas/Antojitos

Tamales, 56

Barbecued Corn on Cobs, 53

Meat Roll, 50

Chilli Peanuts, 49

Cemita, 53

Corn Chips, 46

Corn Fritters, 54

Crisp Flautas, 50

Empanadas, 45

Grilled Fish Steaks, 52

Chicken and Vegetable Brochettes, 48

Tacos, 44

Prawns on Skewers, 43

Appetizers/Entradas/Botanas/Antojitos

Starters in Mexican cuisine are known by various terms. They are called entradas at some places, and botanas or antojitos at other places, but the fact remains that all the vegetarian and non-vegetarian appetizers are colourful and delicious. They are seared, roasted, grilled, sautéd, steamed, baked and fried as per requirement.

1. Prawns on Skewers

You Require: **Cooking Time:** 45 minutes.

Jumbo prawns	12 nos. peeled and de-veined	Ripe tomatoes	2 nos.
Red onions	2 nos.	Peppers–red, yellow or green	½ each
Or small onions	12 nos.		
Green chillies	6 (optional)	Fresh lemon juice	1 tbsp
Olive oil	1 tbsp	Garlic paste	1 tsp
Oregano (dried)	1 tsp	Worcestershire sauce	2 tsp
Salt	1 tsp leveled	Freshly ground pepper	1 tsp
Skewers	4 nos.		

Lemon wedges and **Pico de gallo** to serve with.

Preparation and Cooking:

1. If you are using wooden skewers, soak them in cold water for 30 minutes to 1 hour.
2. Combine together olive oil, lemon juice, Worcestershire sauce, garlic paste, oregano, salt and fresh pepper in a bowl and whisk well. Marinate the prawns in it.
3. Add prawns and toss to coat well. Keep aside at room temperature for 30 minutes to 1 hour.
4. Meanwhile, prepare the vegetables. Cut tomatoes and onions into 1-inch cubes. Remove the seeds and cut peppers also into 1-inch squares.
5. Thread the skewers with vegetables and prawns. Start it with red pepper or onion, pushing it almost all the way down to the end and then add a piece of green pepper, a piece of tomato and then push one jumbo prawn down gently and add one piece of red or yellow pepper; repeat the process and keep alternating the vegetables too. Use 3 prawns in each skewer. Finish threading all the skewers.
6. Heat the gas grill at medium to high temperature or light a hot charcoal fire or heat the convectional electric oven for roasting (use metal skewers for electric oven).

7. Brush the prepared skewers with the remaining marinade and arrange them on the grill. Cook/grill them almost for 6 minutes, turning once in between until the shrimps turn pink and cooked through. In the meantime, the vegetables will also be softened.

Serving: Serve the cooked prawns on skewers hot with Lemon wedges and Pico de Gallo or any other tomato-based sauce.

Provide a fork to each person to slide the vegetables and prawns on to the plate. Slide one-third of the meat and vegetables off the skewer at a time or enjoy eating from the skewer.

Variation: Use chunks of boneless fleshy fish instead of prawns and follow the same procedure.

Tips: The skewers can be assembled and refrigerated hours before cooking, but should be taken out of a refrigerator almost 1 hour before cooking.

If you want to increase the quantity of the dish, just double all the ingredients and follow the process. Cooking time will also be increased.

2. Tacos

Taco is a tortilla folded into a turnover and deep fried. Later, the crisp taco shell is filled with a stuffing and served as a snack.

You Require: **Cooking Time:** 15 minutes for preparation and 30 minutes for frying.

For Tacos:

Corn meal/maize flour	1 cup	Flour	¼ cup
Salt	¼ tsp (opt)	Warm water	to knead the cornmeal
Oil	for frying		

For Filling:

Tomatoes finely chopped	2 nos.	Lettuce chopped	1 head/8 leaves
Pepper green chopped	1 no.	Spring onions chopped	1 cup
Celery chopped	½ cup	Parsley chopped	½ cup
Cheese grated	1 cup		

Or cooked kidney beans and salad ingredients for stuffing.

Enchilada sauce or Tomato salsa to serve with.

Preparation and Cooking for Tacos:

1. Mix cornmeal, salt and flour together with water and turn into soft dough. Divide it into 4 portions.
2. Roll out one portion into a thin disc and with the help of a 2 to 3" biscuit-cutter, take out as many discs as possible. Sprinkle some maize flour while rolling, if required. Prick the discs with a fork lightly. This way finish cutting and pricking all the discs; re-roll the leftovers of the dough and use it too.

3. Heat oil in a small frying pan and fry the discs in it; fry one at a time; place the disc in medium hot oil, and with a pair of tongs, turn it over into half; keep holding till it is crisp, so that the edges do not touch each other; turn the side and then remove it on the kitchen oil-absorbent paper. Finish frying all the discs the same way.
4. Cool and store in an airtight container.

Serving: Fill each Taco with chopped salad; top it with Enchilada sauce and serve it immediately. Or place all the chopped ingredients, taco shells and hot (warmed up) enchilada sauce on the table. Demonstrate how to fill a taco shell; and let all the family members or guests make their own tacos and enjoy them crisp, because some people might like to add more onion/tomato and others more cheese to their tacos. Thus, each one can relish the dish in his or her own way.

Another option is to fill the tacos the way you prefer, top with cheese and arrange in a plate. Heat the plate in a microwave for 30 seconds to 1 minute and eat them hot immediately.

Tips: These days, readymade taco shells are commercially available on the grocery shops but they are quite small in size. Try them if you are short of time.

3. Empanadas

The half moon-shaped corn Empanadas resemble the Italian Calzones, the only difference is that empanadas made of cornmeal are fried, whereas calzones made of pizza dough are baked in the oven.

You Require: **Cooking Time:** 1 hour.

Cornmeal	1 cup	Flour	½ cup
Salt	¼ tsp	Warm water	¾ cup (approximately) to knead
Oil for deep frying		Any veg. or non-veg. filling for stuffing	

Or Combine 1 cup boiled and cubed potatoes or cooked minced meat, 1 cup steamed corn, 1 tbsp fried garlic and onion each, season with salt, pepper, chilli powder and 2 tbsp tomato sauce; sprinkle 1 tbsp cooking oil and heat through for 2 minutes on microwave at high temperature, uncovered; so that all the ingredients absorb the aroma. Sprinkle 3 tbsp chopped coriander and cool.

Preparation and Cooking:

1. Combine all the ingredients of the dough into a bowl or a trove (paraat) and knead with warm water; cover with a moist cloth and keep aside for half-an-hour.
2. Divide the dough into equaize portions; sprinkle a little cornmeal over the surface and roll each portion into a chapatti; place 1 to 1 and ½ tbsp filling on one side of the rolled disc; moisten the edges with water and fold the other half (without filling) over it to get semi-circle shape; press the edges lightly. Finish rolling and stuffing all the empanadas this way.

3. Heat oil for frying in a kadahi/pan and fry all empanadas on medium heat, one by one till golden brown. Drain on oil absorbent paper and serve them hot.

   Serving: Serve Empanadas with any of the salsas as a snack.

   Or serve them with any soup as a mini meal.

Variation: While kneading the dough, add adobo sauce to the empanadas dough and prepare spicy red-coloured empanadas.

4. Corn and Potato Patties with Salsa Mexicana

You Require: **Cooking Time:** 30 minutes.

Boiled and peeled potatoes	800 gm	Corn kernels steamed	200 gm
Fresh corn on the cob grated	1 cup	Cottage cheese or Feta cheese	1 cup
Green chillies	3 nos.	Coriander chopped	¼ cup
Pepper powder	1 tsp	Clove and cinnamon powder	½ tsp
Cooking oil	2 tbsp	Salt	to taste

Red or green salsa to serve with.

Preparation and Cooking:

1. Grate potatoes and crumble cheese.
2. Slit green chillies; remove the seeds and cut them very fine.
3. Mix all the ingredients for the patties in a trove and mash well.
4. Preheat the oven for moderate heat. Apply oil on flat baking tray.
5. Divide the mixture into equal parts. Smear your palms with a little oil; roll and shape each part into patties and place in a baking tray. Finish rolling and shaping all the portions.
6. Brush the patties lightly with oil using a pastry brush and bake in the oven for 20 to 30 minutes.

   Serving: Serve them hot or at room temperature with salsa as a snack.

   Or serve them with salad and soup as a meal.

5. Corn Chips

(Baked)

This is one of the innovative recipes of home-made crisp corn chips which really turns out to be very satisfying.

You Require: **Cooking Time:** 20 minutes.

Cornmeal	1 and ½ cup	Flour	½ cup
Milk powder	¼ cup	Butter	¼ cup
Salt	1 and ½ tsp	White pepper powder	1 tsp
Baking powder	¼ tsp	Warm water to knead with	2 and ½ to 3 cups

Preparation and Cooking:

1. Sieve together cornmeal flour, milk powder, baking powder, salt and pepper powder twoce.
2. Melt the butter and add to the cornmeal flour. Rub with your fingertips till well mixed. Make a hole at the centre of the cornmeal flour. Add half of the warm water and mix the flours. Keep adding a little water at the time of mixing till the mixture turns into soft, pliable dough.
3. Cover it with a moist cloth and let it stand strictly for 5 to 10 minutes.
4. Preheat the oven for moderate heat.
5. Divide the dough into 3 to 4 portions.
6. Roll each portion into a thin chapatti and with a biscuit-cutter, cut it into any shape; take out as many pieces as possible; place them in a baking tray and bake in a moderately hot oven for 15 to 20 minutes. After 10 minutes, take out the baking tray and change the side of the chips. Lightly oil them with a brush and bake till golden brown.
7. Repeat the process with the rest of the portions.
8. If you are baking in a cooking range oven or in a big electric range oven, two trays of the chips can be placed simultaneously for baking. After 10 minutes, when you change the side of the chips, change the place of the trays too. The tray on the upper rack of the oven should be placed on the lower rack and the one on the lower rack on the upper rack, so that the chips on the lower racks are not overcooked.
9. Cool the baked chips thoroughly and store them in an airtight container.

   Or after cutting the chips, fry them in hot oil on medium fire and remove on kitchen oil absorbent paper. Cool and store.

Serving: Serve the crisp 'Corn Chips' with Avocado dip or any other salsa. They are excellent as snacks and the best accompaniments to the soups, stews and drinks.

Variation: You may make chips spicy by adding red chilli powder or oregano to the corn-meal dough.

Tips: Corn chips are also known as Tortillas chips/Nachos.

6. Chicken and Vegetable Brochettes

(Chicken and Vegetables on Skewers)

This dish is an excellent example of grilled food that the Mexicans enjoy since the time immemorial. They are more or less like the famous Indian 'tikkas', but the marinating ingredients are different here.

You Require: **Cooking Time:** 8 to 10 minutes for each batch.

Chicken breasts, boneless	2 nos.	Onions	2 nos.
Red pepper	1 no.	Green pepper	1 no.
Cherry tomatoes	12 to 24 nos.	Mushrooms	12 to 24 nos.

For marinade:

Lemon juice	2 tbsp	Olive oil	2 tbsp
Oregano dry	1 tsp	Worcestershire sauce	1 tbsp
Freshly ground black pepper	1 tsp	No salt or salt to taste	
Bamboo or metal skewers	12 nos.		

Preparation and Cooking:

1. Wash and cut chicken breasts into 1 and ½-inch cubes.
2. Halve the peppers and cut them too into cubes.
3. Peel the onions and cut them into quarters.
4. Remove the stems of the mushroom and clean them with a wet kitchen towel.
5. Combine all the ingredients for marinade in a bowl and mix thoroughly; put chicken pieces in it and coat well; add the vegetables too in the marinade; toss well and keep aside for 2 hours.

   Or marinate chicken and keep it under refrigeration for 6 to 8 hours and take it out 1 hour before cooking; add vegetables and toss well.
6. Do not cut cherry tomatoes.
7. Soak bamboo skewers in cold water at least for 30 minutes to 1 hour.
8. Heat a gas grill to medium high temperature or light a hot charcoal fire.
9. Thread the skewers with chicken meat and vegetables according to the preference of the colour. Use 2 to 3 layers of onions at a time. Start with onion and push it almost to the end of the skewer. Follow it with chicken and vegetables. Repeat threading chicken and vegetables and finish off the skewer with a cherry tomato. Brush the skewers with the remaining marinade.

10. Grill the skewers, turning them twice at least till the chicken is cooked through and the vegetables are softened. Each batch may take 8 to 10 minutes to be cooked.
11. Serve them on skewer or slide them in a serving plate with a fork.

Serving: Serve them as appetizers with any salsa or sour cream dip.

Or serve them with Mexican Green rice and tomato-based Tortilla soup as a meal.

Variation: Use paneer pieces instead of chicken and go ahead.

Tips: Skewers can be assembled in advance before cooking and refrigerated.

The remaining marinade can be transformed into a dip; mix ¼ cup water and 1 tsp leveled corn flour with the marinade and boil for a few seconds. Serve it with grilled meat and vegetables.

7. Chilli Peanuts

Chilli peanuts are commonly served in each Mexican bar and restaurant along with drinks as a ready made snack. They are also used as one of the ingredients in the preparation of certain dressings for salads, dips and crust for frying fish, etc.

You Require: **Cooking Time:** 15 to 20 minutes.

Unsalted dry roasted peanuts	2 cups	Lemon juice	1 tbsp
Vegetable/olive oil	1 tbsp	Salt	1 tsp
Mild chilli powder or Kashmiri mirch	1 tsp		

Preparation and cooking:

1. Preheat the oven to 180 degrees Celsius.
2. Except peanuts, mix all the ingredients in a bowl and toss the peanuts until well coated evenly. At this stage, the peanuts will appear slightly wet.
3. Spread them in an even layer in a baking sheet/tray and bake for 15 to 20 minutes or until the peanuts are dry and spices are lightly toasted.
4. Avoid baking them in very hot oven, otherwise the nuts will be burnt and bitter in taste.
5. Remove the tray from the oven and let the peanuts cool completely. Store at room temperature in an airtight container; they will be fresh for more than a fortnight (two weeks).

Note: If they become a little soggy, reheat them in an oven for 5 to 7 minutes.

Serving: Serve them as a starter with drinks in any gathering.

8. Meat Roll

(Baked Minced Meat Roll)

This baked dish is like a meat loaf – very light and tasty, and if consumed with a fresh-crisp vegetable salad, a light soup and some bread, it makes an excellent satisfying meal. It is cooked with the baked-steamed technique.

You Require: **Cooking Time:** 1 hour.

Mutton/chicken mince	500 gm	Red pepper finely chopped	2 tbsp
Green pepper finely chopped	2 tbsp	Yellow pepper finely chopped	2 tbsp
Oregano dry	1 tsp	Egg	1 large or 2 small
Pepper freshly ground	1and ½ tsp	Garlic paste	1 tsp
Worcestershire sauce	a few drops	Breadcrumbs fresh	1 cup
Salt	to taste		

One 24 – inch long piece of aluminium foil

One roasting tin

Preparation and Cooking:

1. Preheat the oven for moderate heat.
2. Combine minced, chopped peppers and garlic in a bowl.
3. Beat eggs and pour over the mince.
4. Add salt, pepper, oregano, Worcestershire sauce and bread crumbs.
5. Mix the ingredients with your hands and shape it into a big roll.
6. Put the meat mixture on aluminium sheet, shape the roll and wrap it in the foil from all sides. Then transfer it to a roasting tin. Add hot water to come half way up the sides of the roll, and bake in the preheated oven for about 40 to 45 minutes or until cooked through.
7. Remove the roll from the oven and cool. Remove the foil and slice the meat diagonally.

Serving: Serve it with any Mexican salad as a starter; and with Cilantro Soup and Spinach and Mushroom salad as a light meal.

Tips: Meat roll can be baked in advance and chilled. It can be sliced just before serving. Leftover sliced meat roll can also be used as one of the sandwich fillings. Use your favorite salsa or finely chopped salad along with cheese to make burgers or sandwiches.

9. Crisp Flautas

(Flautas)

'Flauta' means a flute in Spanish. Flautas, in fact, are rolled tacos. They are filled with veg. or non-veg. filling and rolled tightly like flute, and later either shallow fried (as in this recipe) or brushed with oil and baked in the oven till warm and crisp. They are served as little munchies and as appetizers. They also form a part of the meal when served with soup and salad. Any type of leftover meat can be nicely consumed as a stuffing for this dish.

You Require: **Cooking Time:** 35 to 40 minutes.

6-inch thinner corn tortillas 8 nos.

Vegetable oil for frying

For Filling:

Chopped and par boiled vegetables 2 cups

Or cooked or shredded chicken 1 and ½ cup

Olive oil	2 tbsp	Onion chopped	1 small
Garlic chopped fine	2 cloves	Jalapeno chopped fine	1 tbsp
Large tomato	1 no.	Bay leaf	1 no.
Red chilli sauce	1 tbsp leveled	Sugar	½ tsp
Dry oregano	¼ tsp	Dried thyme	a pinch
Salt	to taste		

To serve with: Shredded lettuce, Sour cream and Grated cheese (opt)

Preparation and Cooking:

1. Cut tomato into small pieces and save the juices.
2. Heat olive oil over medium heat in a pan/kadai; and add onion and cook till transparent, almost for 3 minutes.
3. Add garlic and jalapeno and cook for 1 minute; add tomato with its liquid and stir well. Add bay leaf and salt and keep stirring.
4. Add chilli sauce, oregano and thyme; cook till most of the liquid has evaporated and the mixture is slightly thickened.
5. Add vegetables or shredded chicken and stir. The filling should be moist but not either wet or too dry.
6. Discard the bay leaf and check the salt. Remove from fire and cool to room temperature.
7. Wrap the tortillas in a kitchen towel and warm up to 30 seconds in a microwave. Keep them wrapped. Or warm up tortillas on lightly oiled griddle over a medium fire.
8. Spread 2 tablespoons filling in the centre of a tortilla; fold one edge of the tortilla over the filling and with the help of your fingers, start rolling it neatly into a compact flute shape.. Roll another tortilla the same way and place 2 flautas side by side with their loose edges touching at the centre. Pass 2 toothpicks through the centre of the flautas to hold them together. Repeat the process with the remaining tortillas to convert them into flautas.

9. Heat ½-cup oil in a frying pan and place 2 pairs of flautas carefully in it; cook until the underside is lightly browned and crisp; turn them carefully and change the side and cook the second side too. Remove them in a plate lined with paper napkins to remove excess oil. Repeat the process with rest of the rolled flautas too.

Serving: Remove the toothpicks and serve 1 pair of flautas in a plate lined with shredded lettuce and spoon on enough of the salsa to coat the flautas; add a spoon of sour cream and sprinkle 1 tbsp grated cheese.

Tips: Flautas can be formed several hours in advance, covered with a cling film and stored under refrigeration. Take them out 30 minutes before cooking.

10. Grilled Fish Steaks

An excellent source of high-quality protein, tuna is rich in a variety of important nutrients, minerals, magnesium and potassium, vitamin B and omega 3 fatty acids. This preparation is not only easy to cook, but also one of the outstanding foods. While served with delicious salsa, not only it enhances the flavour of the fish but it also maintains the immune system.

You Require:

Cooking Time: 20 minutes for preparation and 15 to 20 minutes for cooking.

Tuna fish steaks	4 nos. 100 gm each	Olive oil	1 tbsp
Or steaks of any other Indian fish		Lemon juice	1 tbsp
Garlic, finely crushed	1 clove	Salt	to taste
Freshly ground pepper	1 tsp	Lemon/Lime wedges	

Pico de Gallo or Salsa Mexicana to serve with.

Preparation and Cooking:

1. Combine oil, lemon juice, salt and pepper in a small bowl and mix.
2. Brush the fish steaks with it; cover the fish and stand it for 20 to 30 minutes.
3. Meantime, prepare the salsa.
4. Heat a grill and cook fish steaks under it, turning the sides after 3 to 4 minutes and brushing them with a little more oil till the steaks are cooked through, still moist and golden in appearance.
5. Transfer the steaks to a warm plate to serve.

Serving: You may serve one steak each individually in a plate lined with lettuce leaves and salsa over it.

Tips: Indian variety of fish, Surmai and Rohu, are good choice for this preparation.

You may cook this dish in a preheated ridged griddle pan over a gas stove also.

Note: Preparation time is not included in cooking time.

11. Barbecued Corn on Cobs

The vendor style roasted corn-on-cobs are very popular in Mexico as an appetizer or a snack. This street food is ideal for barbecue parties.

You require: **Cooking Time:** 30 minutes.

Corn on cobs	4 nos.	Mayonnaise	2 tbsp
Garlic paste	½ tsp	Green chilli paste	½ to 1 tsp
Lemon juice	1 tbsp	Or Indian green chutney	1 tbsp
Salt	¼ tsp	Cheese grated	¼ cup

Red chilli powder for sprinkling on top.

Preparation and Cooking:

1. Combine mayonnaise, garlic and chilli pastes, salt and lemon juice together in a bowl; mix and keep under refrigeration.
2. Husk the corn cobs; remove the thicker layers of husk and leave the soft lower part still attached to the cobs. Gather these husks together and tie with a piece of twine/thread, so that holding the warm roasted corncobs and eating them becomes easier.
3. Remove all the silk from the corn on the cobs.
4. Either place the corn on the hot grill for roasting or roast it on naked flame of the gas, turning often, until the corn is evenly roasted and charred at places.
5. Mix grated cheese, with mayonnaise mixture and spread each ear of corn with a thin layer of mayonnaise. Hold each ear of corn and season it with chilli powder.

Serving: Serve one ear of corn each with additional salt and chilli powder. Each person can add more chilli and salt, if desired.

12. Cemita

(Mexican Sandwich with Avocado, Cheese and Chicken)

In some parts of Mexico, Cemita is a kind of bread but in the city of Pubeta, Cemita is a sandwich made with chicken, beef or pork cutlets coated with seasoned bread crumbs and fried or simply made with ham and cheese.

You Require:		Assembling Time: 30 minutes, if chicken is precooked.	
Hot dog buns, large	4 nos.	Breaded or fried chicken pieces	4 to 6 nos.
Ripe avocado, pitted and sliced	1 nos.	Guacamole	½ cup
Adobo sauce	½ cup	Pickled jalapeno strips	8 nos.
Pickled red onions	1 recipe		
Cheese, grated	½ cup	Lettuce	1 head
Or cheese slices	4 nos.	Cilantro sprigs	Olive oil

Preparation and cooking:

1. Split the rolls, place on a baking tray/sheet, and warm in the oven, until softened.
2. Warm the fried chicken pieces.
3. Assemble the sandwich: Spread adobo sauce on the cut sides of all the softened rolls; place 1 lettuce leaf, each on the 4 portions of the rolls; spread avocado slices on the buns evenly or pour guacamole; place one cheese slice on each one or sprinkle grated cheese and top with the warm chicken. Mount the cilantro sprigs over the chicken and drizzle olive oil over the greens. Top with pickled onions and chilli strips, cover with tops (the other halves) of the buns and press slightly and gently.

Serving: Cut the sandwich in half before serving, so that it is easier to handle while eating.

Note: This sandwich is a meal in itself as breaded and fried chicken cutlet in it makes it sumptuous.

Tips: How to bread the chicken and fry it:

Cut the 1 skinless chicken breast into thick slices; cover each piece with a thick plastic sheet and pound with a meat mallet/flattener to inch thickness. Spread ½ cup flour in a plate, sprinkle 1 tbsp of the salt, 1 tbsp dried oregano and ½ tsp chilli powder over it. Beat 1 egg very well. Spread ½-cup bread crumbs in a separate plate. Coat the chicken pieces with seasoned flour evenly; tap off excess flour; turn the chicken into the egg to coat evenly; place on the bread crumbs, turning and patting gently, so that all the pieces are coated well; pour ½-inch layer of vegetable oil in a pan and heat it over on high flame; lower the heat to medium and fry the chicken pieces for almost 4 to 5 minutes or until the chicken is golden brown. Remove and drain on an oil absorbent paper. Chicken can be fried beforehand and kept at the room temperature. Chicken cooked in advance can be warmed up before use.

13. Corn Fritters

Crispy, crusty, golden corn fritters are one of the handy snacks and seem delicious when served with honey.

You require:		Cooking Time: 40 to 45 minutes.	
Flour	1 and ½ cup	Maize flour	¾ cup
Corn kernels	2 cup	Baking powder	2 and ½ tsp leveled
Or Cream style corn	2 cup	Salt	2 tsp leveled
Pepper powder	½ tsp	Chilli flakes	1 tsp
Dry oregano	1 tsp	Eggs	2 nos.
Melted butter	1 tbsp	Or Olive oil	1 tbsp
Cooking oil for frying			

Preparation and Cooking:

1. Coarsely grind the corn with ½ cup water, if using corn kernels.
2. Sieve flour, maize flour, salt and baking powder together in a bowl. Add pepper, chilli flakes and oregano.
3. Beat eggs thoroughly. Melt butter. Add liquids to the dry ingredients. Add ground corn or cream-style corn to the mixture and mix well. Sprinkle a few drops of water, if the mixture is too dry. Cover and keep aside for 20 minutes.
4. Heat fat for frying and lower the heat.
5. Drop a few teaspoonfuls of mixture into hot fat; increase the heat and fry the fritters until golden brown. Drain on an oil absorbent paper.

   Serving: Serve the fritters warm with honey.

   You may serve some fried bacon too with the fritters.

14. Veg Torta

Torta is a unique Mexican word for a variety of sandwiches. Tortas can be made with a variety of breads, but, commonly, it is made with flattish roll that is soft and porous inside and crusty outside. A torta can be stuffed with almost anything. Traditionally, in most of the cases, bread is spread with refried black beans or pinto beans and sour cream/mayonnaise; and then stuffed with any of the meats of the choice. They also spread slices of ripe avocado, pickled jalapeno and white onions, etc. Thus, the layers result in awful flavour and textures. Such tortas are meals in themselves.

You Require:		Assembling Time: 30 minutes	
Hot dog buns, large	4 nos.	Vegetable cutlets	4 to 6 nos.
Refried black beans	2 cup	Or Adobo sauce	½ cup
Pickled jalapeno strips	8 nos.	Pickled red onion	1 recipe

Ripe avocado, pitted and sliced	½ cup	Cheese slices	4 nos.
Or cheese grated		Cilantro sprigs	
Lettuce	1 head	Olive oil or sour cream	

Preparation and Cooking:

1. Split the rolls, place on a baking tray/sheet, and warm in the oven until softened.
2. Warm the cutlets.
3. *Assemble the sandwich*: Spread refried beans or adobo sauce or both on the cut sides of all the softened rolls; place 1 lettuce leaf each on the 4 portions of the rolls; spread avocado slices on the buns evenly; place one cheese slice on each one or sprinkle grated cheese; and top with the warm cutlet. Mount the cilantro sprigs over the cutlet and drizzle olive oil or sour cream over the greens. Top with pickled onions and jalapeno strips, cover with tops (the other halves) of the buns and press lightly and gently.

Serving: Cut the sandwich in half before serving, so that it is easier to handle while eating. Serve soup with it.

Note: This sandwich is a meal in itself as the cutlet and salad in it make it quite sumptuous.

15. Cheese and Chilli Morsels

(Tamales)

Tamales are one of those various snacks that are steamed. Tamale dough disks are stuffed with vegetarian/non-vegetarian filling; then wrapped in corn husks and tied with thread, they are placed in a steamer for cooking.

You Require: **Cooking Time:** 1 hour 30 minutes.

Corn husks	20		
For tamale dough:			
Butter	100 gm	Corn meal	500 gm
Baking powder	1 and ½ tsp	Water	½ cup
For filling:			
Cooking oil	1 tbsp	Green chillies chopped	2 nos.
Oregano dry	1 tsp	Garlic crushed	1 clove
Cottage cheese crumbled	1 cup		
Mixed veggies grated	½ cup	Or Chicken mince	200 gm
Flour	1 tbsp	Tomato puree	1 tbsp

Note: When using chicken, don't use cottage cheese; you may use vegetables with chicken or cheese.

Preparation and Cooking:

1. Place corn husks in a large bowl and soak in warm water for 30 minutes.
2. Meantime, make tamale dough. Place butter in a bowl and beat till light and creamy.
3. Add cornmeal and baking powder; stir in water or stock and mix to combine well. Continue beating till mixture is smooth. Cover and keep aside.
4. Make filling. Heat oil in a pan; add chillies and garlic and stir; add chicken and cook for 5 minutes or till all the liquid evaporates; sprinkle flour over it and mix; add puree and mix thoroughly. Season it with oregano.
5. Remove corn husks from water and pat them dry with kitchen towel.
6. Take 3 tbsp tamale dough on your palm; roll and flatten it; place 1 tbsp filling in the centre and close the edges over it. Lightly press it with the fingertips to flatten it and place on a corn husk. Now, fold corn husk around the dough; wrap the husk around the parcel in the opposite direction and finally tie a thread to secure it.
7. Repeat the process with remaining corn husks, dough and filling.
8. Place tamales in a steamer/rice colander over a pan of boiling water and steam for 40 to 45 minutes or till cooked.

Serving: Serve the steamed tamales with any Red salsa.

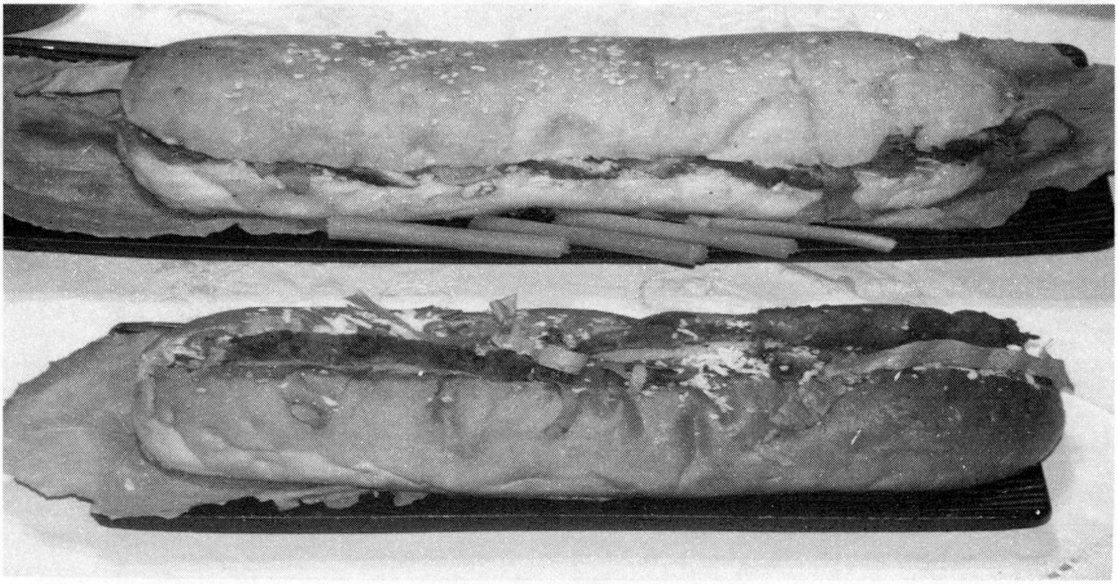

Veg Torta

Corn Patties with Salsa

Sopas/Soups

Mutton Stew with Adobo, 62

Avocado Cold Soup, 63

Beans and Meat Soup, 61

Beetroot and Carrot Soup, 64

Black-beans Soup, 65

Cilantro Soup, 71

Corn Dumplings in Soup, 69

Walnut Soup, 68

Milpa Soup, 66

Mutton Stew with Adobo, 62

Roasted Corn and Cilantro Soup, 71

Chicken Broth with Avocado, Chickpeas and Carrots, 67

Corn Tortilla Soup with Tomatoes, 63

Sopas/Soups

Mexican soups are delicious, hearty and full of nourishment. Flavourful vegetable/ meat stocks or broths with pureed tomatoes, garlic and onion, seasoned with fresh herbs, coriander, lime, chillies and cheese – Mexicans have created a broad base for a brilliant variety of soups. Their presentation, is spectacular. A big steaming bowl of soup is a prelude to a traditional Mexican meal.

1. Fresh Corn Chowder with Roasted Peppers

(Crema de Elote)

This is one of the most popular soups of Mexico. Its smooth, rich texture, punctuated with green chilli and fresh cheese, makes it special. Usually, a large Mexican soup is a meal in itself. Mostly, the lighter soups are served before the main course and the rustic classic to make a meal on. Heavy ones are just right to be served for informal supper or winter lunch, together with some of the delicious 'masa' snacks.

You Require: **Cooking Time:** 40 to 45 minutes.

Fresh corn on the cobs	3 ears	Onion chopped	1 no. small
Or frozen corn	2 and ½ to 3 cups	Garlic minced	1 tsp heaped
White/unsalted butter	4 tbsp	Poblano/long green chillies	2 to 3 nos.
Corn-flour	2 tbsp leveled	Milk	2 cups
Fresh cream	1 cup	Salt	to taste
Feta cheese/other cheese	1 cup	Parsley chopped for garnishing	2 tbsp

Preparation and Cooking:

1. Roast, peel, seed and cut chillies into strips.
2. Grate corn on the cobs. Place grated corn or frozen corn in the electric blender or a processor.
3. Heat half of the butter in a pan over medium fire and fry chopped onion in it for 2 minutes; and add garlic paste. Stir and cook for 1 minute more and remove from fire.
4. Scrape and add to the corn mixture in the blender. Add corn-flour and ¼ to ½ cup water and blend until smooth.
5. Melt the remaining butter in a pan over medium heat; add pureed corn and cook, stirring constantly, until quite thick.
6. Mix the milk in it thoroughly and simmer for 15 minutes on low fire.

7. Strain the soup through a medium mesh sieve (not so fine), add more milk, if the soup is very thick.
8. Rinse the pan with water, pour the soup in it and return it to fire. Stir in the chilli strips and cream. Season the soup with salt and simmer for 10 minutes over low heat, stirring often.

Note: The consistency of the soup should not be thicker than the heavy cream, otherwise dilute it and add a little more milk while serving.

Serving: Ladle the soup in small (warmed) soup bowls and garnish with chopped parsley and crumbled cheese. Serve it hot immediately.

Tips: Though in Mexico it is made with non-sweet field corn but due to the availability of American sweet corn everywhere, people have started using it. Indian corn on the cobs is just ideal for this preparation. If properly covered and refrigerated, this soup lasts for several days. Reheat it on slow fire, adding a little more milk to thin it.

Traditional variations:

Add 1 large roasted, peeled and chopped tomato along with the chillies.

All or half the milk can be replaced with chicken stock/broth.

Contemporary ideas:

Prepare 1 recipe, with 1 red and 1 poblano pepper (roasted, peeled and chopped) and with 1 roasted, peeled and diced tomato. Before serving add ½ to 1 cup cleaned and de-veined shrimps to the boiling soup and cook for 3 minutes more. Serve garnished with feta cheese.

2. Aromatic Coriander Soup

(Cilantro soup)

Cilantro belongs to coriander family and is somewhat another name and variety of coriander. It makes lovely soup, which is light and aromatic.

You Require: **Cooking Time:** 15 minutes.

Coriander chopped	2 cups	Potato boiled and cubed	1 no medium
Bay leaf	2 nos.	Cinnamon stick	1" piece
Milk	1 cup	Water	4 cups
Butter	1 tbsp	Salt-n-pepper	to taste
Taste maker/Soup cube	1 no.		

Or Flavourful stock instead of water (veg/non-veg.)

Preparation and Cooking:

1. Heat butter in a pan; add cinnamon and bay leaf; stir for a while and add coriander, boiled potato and 2 cups of water; bring it to the boiling point and then let it simmer for 5 minutes.

2. Add milk and let it cool. Meantime, dissolve soup cube in 2 cups of warm water.
3. Pass the coriander mixture through a blender and strain through a fine mesh, so that the roughage of bay leaves and cinnamon does not spoil the smoothness of the coriander puree. Mix the dissolved cube mixture with coriander mixture and heat it thoroughly either in a microwave or in a pan.
4. Adjust seasonings, if required, and serve.

Serving: Serve the refreshing green Cilantro soup with any accompaniments like Corn chips/ Soup sticks or Empanadas, etc.

Tips: Do not overcook Cilantro/coriander for soup, it will lose the colour.

3. Beans and Meat Soup

Well-flavoured, a thick Mexican soup that accompanies very well with a good vegetable salad and plain tortillas.

You Require: **Cooking Time:** 35 minutes micro cooking.

Kidney beans 1 cup soaked and cooked

Note: Soak 1 cup of kidney beans in warm water for 6 to 8 hours or overnight; cook in a pressure cooker with 4 cups water and 2 tsp salt for 30 to 35 minutes before use.

Boneless mutton	300 gm	Tomato puree	¼ cup
Onion chopped	1 small	Garlic chopped	1 tbsp
Butter	2 tsp	Salt pepper	to taste
Red chilli powder	¼ tsp (opt)	Parsley chopped	2 tbsp
Water/mutton stock	5 cups	Bouquet - garni	a small bag

Preparation and Cooking:

1. Mash the cooked kidney beans with a wooden spoon till mushy and keep aside.
2. Cut mutton into ½ inch small cubes.
3. Combine mutton pieces, ginger powder, bouquet garni and 2 cups of water in pressure cooker; cover and cook first on high flame till cooker starts whistling, then lower the heat and cook it for 20 minutes. Let the pressure drop itself. Open the cooker.
4. In a pan heat butter and sauté onion and garlic in it. Add boiled beans with its liquid and ½ cup water. Cover and cook for 5 minutes on. Mash the beans with a wooden spoon once again.
5. Now remove the bag of bouquet garni from meat and squeeze its liquid into the soup and discard the bag. Add cooked and mashed beans, onion-garlic, grated cheese, tomato puree, salt and pepper to the soup and cook for 5 minutes on high fire and then on low fire for 10 minutes. Check the seasonings. Add chilli powder and stir properly.

Note: Soak 1 cup of kidney beans in warm water for 6 to 8 hours or overnight; cook in pressure cooker with 4 cups water and 1 tsp salt for 30 to 35 minutes before use.

Serving: Garnish the soup with grated cheese and chopped parsley; and serve it hot with toasted Bread or Tortillas.

Tips: Bouquet garni is a small cheese cloth bag that contains whole spices, e.g. 10 to 12 peppercorns, 2 cardamoms, 1inch stick cinnamon, 6 to 8 cloves and any other dry herbs. You may add 1 bay leaf too. After initial cooking, the aromatic juices of the bag are squeezed in the dish and bag is discarded.

4. Mutton Stew with Adobo

(Mutton Stew)

Spicy chilli flavoured mutton stew, an excellent accompaniment to rice and tortillas, makes a sumptuous meal. If you don't want to eat much with this tasty stew, you may just enjoy it with corn chips or tacos.

You Require: **Cooking Time:** 35 minutes.

Boneless mutton	500 gm	Adobo	¼ cup
Flour	2 tbsp	Or Kashmiri chillies	5 nos.
Butter/olive oil	3 to 4 tbsp	Onions chopped	2 nos.
Garlic chopped	1 tbsp	Tomato puree	¼ cup
Oregano	1 tsp	Cumin powder	1 tsp
Salt	2 tsp leveled	Coriander chopped fine	¼ cup

Preparation and Cooking:

1. Break, deseed, toast and soak red chillies in ¼ cup water for 20 minutes.
2. Meantime, wash and cut mutton in 1-inch small pieces; sprinkle flour and 1 tsp salt over it, mix and let it stand for 30 minutes.
3. Add mutton and stir till well coated with oil; add chilli paste and cook for 2 minutes on high flame.
4. Add rest of the ingredients except coriander and cook for another 5 minutes.
5. Pour 1 cup water over meat and stir well. Sprinkle half the coriander over it and close the lid of the pressure cooker. Lower the heat after the first whistle and cook for 20 to 25 minutes to get the well-cooked meat with thick sauce. Remove from fire and let the pressure drop itself.

Serving: Garnish the yummy 'Chilli Mutton Stew' with remaining coriander and serve it hot with Rice/Tortillas or bread, etc.

Variation: Add scraped baby potatoes and carrots cut into cubes to the stew.

5. Corn Tortilla Soup with Tomatoes

This is one of the most delicious soups of central Mexico. It is flavoured with 'epazote' sprigs, if available, otherwise coriander sprigs are used. It is garnished with cheese, avocado and chilli rings. It is also known as 'Aztec' soup. This healthy soup is rich in vitamins and minerals.

You Require: **Cooking Time:** 45 minutes.

Ripe tomatoes	2 nos.	Garlic clove chopped	1 no.
Onion chopped	1 no. small	Cooking oil	1 tbsp
Chicken stock	6 cups	Coriander sprigs	3 nos.
Chilli rings	from 2 nos.	Feta cheese/paneer	100 gm crumbled
Avocado (ripe)	1 no.	Salt	to taste
Freshly ground pepper	to taste	Tortillas	4 nos.
Fried or baked tortilla strips from 4 tortillas			

Preparation and Cooking:

1. Skin and deseed tomatoes.
2. Stone/pit, peel and dice avocado.
3. Place tomato, onion and garlic in a blender and puree. Add ¼ cup water/stock, if required.
4. Heat oil in a large pan; add tomato mixture and cook for 2 to 3 minutes. Lower the heat and let the mixture simmer for 10 minutes. Add stock and bring it to the boiling point.
5. Add coriander or epazote sprigs, lower the heat and simmer for 15 minutes or so. Discard the sprigs and season the soup with salt and pepper.
6. Preheat oven on 180 degrees Celsius.
7. Brush tortillas with oil from both the sides; cut into strips and spread on greased baking tray and bake until golden brown.
8. Cut the chillies into ¼-inch rings, discarding the seeds; and fry them in hot oil till crisp. Drain on oil absorbent paper.

Serving: Divide the hot soup in individual cups and garnish with crisp tortilla strips, cheese, avocado and chilli rings; and serve immediately.

Tips: You may cut totillas into strips without being oiled and deep fry instead of baking.

6. Avocado Cold Soup

This delicious soup is just ideal for summer months as it is very refreshing when it is scorching hot outside.

You Require:		**Preparation Time:** 15 minutes and chilling time extra.	
Avocado ripe	1 no.	Onion chopped	1 no. small
Green chilli chopped	1 no. (opt)	Garlic chopped	1 tsp
Lemon juice	1 to 2 tsp	Chopped coriander	2 tbsp
Veg./non-veg. stock	3 cups	Salt and freshly crushed pepper	to taste

Preparation:

1. Cut avocado into half; stone and chop in small pieces.
2. Place avocado, chopped onion, garlic, green chilli and lemon juice in a mixer/food processor. Add 1 cup water and blend well till smooth.
3. Remove the mixture in a bowl, add rest of the stock and season well with salt, half the pepper powder and half the chopped coriander.
4. Cover the bowl and chill the soup under refrigeration till served.

Serving: Serve it chilled in individual bowls, garnished with coriander and black pepper.

Tips: You should always cover the avocado preparation with a lid or cling wrap while storing it under refrigeration as avocado tends to change colour and turns brown.

7. Beetroot and Carrot Soup

(Tubers' Soup)

An excellent tuber soup; not only it is packed with healthy nutrients, vitamin A and potassium, but its enchanting colour is also an aesthetical feast for the eye.

You Require:		**Cooking Time:** 35 to 40 minutes.	
Beetroots	3 nos.	Carrots	5 nos. medium
Onion chopped fine	1 no large	Garlic chopped fine	1 tbsp
Water	6 cups	Soup cube	1 no.
Green chilli	1 no.	Cheese grated	¼ cup
Bay leaf	1 no.	Or Feta cheese crumbled	
Butter	2 tbsp	Salt	to taste
Freshly crushed pepper	to taste	Parsley chopped	2 tbsp
Roasted sesame seeds	2 tbsp		

Preparation and Cooking:

1. Wash, clean and roughly chop beetroots and carrots; cook them with 3 cups of water and green chilli till soft. Add one sprig of parsley and bay leaf when vegetables are cooking. Cool; discard bay leaf and parsley sprig and pass the vegetables through a liquidizer.

   Or

Steam the vegetables with ¼ cup of water in a microwave for 6 minutes, covered. Let them stand for 5 minutes. Remove from the microwave, pour 2 cups water over it and strain. Save the liquid. Pass the vegetables through a liquidizer; mix the strained liquid and stir properly.

2. Heat butter and sauté chopped onion and garlic in it. Add pureed root vegetables and rest of the water. Cook for 10 minutes on medium fire.
3. Dissolve soup cube in ½ cup water and add to the soup. You may add ½ cup water more if the soup appears very thick.
4. Divide the hot soup in 6 soup bowls.

Serving: Serve the soup hot, garnished with grated or crumbled cheese, chopped parsley and roasted sesame seeds.

Corn tortillas/Cheese La Casa Dias or Soup sticks are the best accompaniments.

Tips: You may save cooking time by softening the vegetables in a microwave.

8. Black-beans Soup

Since beans are one of the staple ingredients of Mexican cuisine, they are eaten in all the possible ways. The black beans soup is one of the favourite ones; it becomes special when served with crisp tortilla strips; and garnished with feta cheese and oregano on the top.

You Require: **Cooking Time:** 1 hour 30 minutes

Dried black beans	1 and ½ cup	Water	8 cups
Onion cut into halves	1 no.	Garlic	5 cloves
Vegetable stock	2 cups	Tomatoes	2 nos.
Onion chopped	1 no. small	Fresh epazote sprig	1 no. (opt)
Salt	1 tsp	Olive oil	1 tbsp
Red chilli deseeded	1 no.	Tortillas	2 nos.
Oil for brushing	1 tbsp	Feta cheese/soft paneer	½ cup
Oregano dried	1 tsp		

Preparation and Cooking:

1. Clean, wash and soak black beans in plenty of water for 8 hours or overnight. Drain and rinse. Place them in a pressure cooker and put half the measured water and pressure cook for 20 minutes.
2. Let the pressure drop itself; add rest of the water, onion cut into halves, 3 cloves garlic, epazote and salt; bring it to the boiling point and reduce the heat. Cook for another 20 to 30 minutes and remove the epazote, onion and garlic cloves.

Or

3. Simmer beans for 1 and ½ hours or till the beans are soft. Remove onion, epazote sprig and garlic. Mash half the beans nicely with cooking water with the help of wooden spoon; mix rest of the beans and the stock.
4. Puree tomatoes, chopped onion and remaining garlic. Slice the red chilli fine and keep aside.
5. Heat olive oil, cook tomato puree in it for 3 minutes on high fire; reduce the heat and then simmer for another 5 minutes.
6. Add tomato mixture to the bean mixture and simmer for 10 minutes. Add ½ cup water if soup is too thick. Check the seasoning.
7. Meantime, brush the tortillas with oil, cut into thin strips, spread on the baking sheet and bake in a preheated oven till crisp and golden.

Serving: Serve the soup in individual soup plates, topped with a few tortilla strips. Sprinkle over crumbled feta cheese, chilli strips and oregano.

Serve it hot immediately.

9. Milpa Soup

(Corn and Vegetables' Soup)

This delicious vegetable soup is packed with vitamins, minerals, and so many other nutrients that help to strengthen the immune system as vegetables are a good source of dietary fibre. 'Milpa, in fact, is the term used for a corn field where a great variety of vegetables and fruits are also cultivated."This soup is one of the pre-Hispanic dishes that use vegetables harvested in the milpa".

You Require: **Cooking Time:** 35 to 40 minutes.

Corn kernels	1 and ½ cup	Courgettes/zucchini	2 nos.
Beans	1 cups cut into pieces	Mushrooms	1 cup (opt)
Poblano chillies	2 no	Tomato skinned	1 large
Or Jalapeno chillies	2 to 3 nos.	Onion chopped fine	1 small
Garlic chopped fine	1 clove	Olive/cooking oil	2 tbsp
Epazote	2 large sprigs if available	Or Coriander sprigs	3 to 4 nos.
Salt	to taste	Fresh ground pepper	1 tsp or to taste
Veg. or chicken stock	6 cups		

Preparation and Cooking:

1. Roast the chillies on the naked high gas flame, turning frequently with a tong. Roast until the skin of the chillies is charred.
2. Now place the chillies in a plastic bag, wrap the bag in the kitchen napkin and leave to

sweat for 15 to 20 minutes. Remove the skin of the chillies with a knife; cut them open; discard the stem and the seeds and rinse the chillies under running water; pat dry with a dry napkin and slice.

3. Chop the skinned tomato; cut zucchini into strips and mushroom into quarters.
4. Heat oil in a large pan and sauté onion and garlic in it, add chillies, corn and remaining vegetables; and cook for 2 minutes on high fire, stirring all the time.
5. Add coriander or epazote sprigs and stock together, bring it to the boiling point; reduce heat and simmer for 15 minutes to 20 minutes or till the vegetables are crunchy soft. Remove the sprigs.
6. Add salt and pepper and check the taste for perfection.

Serving: Serve the soup hot in individual plates or soup bowls with Chilli Croutons.

10. Chicken Broth with Avocado, Chickpeas and Carrots

"Soups are an integral part of the Mexican diet. In central Mexico, lunch generally starts with a soup followed by rice and a main course with vegetables".

This broth is a highly nutritious combination of chicken and vegetables. Chicken, vegetables and chickpeas provide protein, vitamins and minerals, such as calcium, potassium and iron. The soup also contains antiseptic and diuretic properties.

You Require: **Cooking Time:** 45 minutes.

Boneless chicken breast	1 no.	Chickpeas boiled	2 cup
Carrots	2 no medium	Avocado	1 no.
Chilli strips	from 1 jalapeno	Roasted garlic	2 cloves
Onion chopped fine	1 no.	Olive oil	2 tbsp
Salt and pepper	to taste	Water/chicken stock	7 cup
Coriander chopped	2 tbsp for garnishing		
Lime	1 no. (opt)		

Preparation and Cooking:

1. Place the chicken breast in the saucepan; pour stock/water over it and bring it to the boiling point. Simmer it for about 30 minutes or till the chicken is cooked.
2. Remove the chicken from the stock and save the stock. Cool the chicken and shred it.
3. Clean and dice carrots. Stone peel and dice avocado. Cut lime into wedges and keep aside.
4. Heat the oil in a large pan; sauté onion and carrots in it till onion is almost transparent. Add garlic and stir for a while.
5. Pour the reserved stock and chickpeas, and simmer for 15 minutes.
6. Season it with salt and pepper.
7. Add shredded chicken and chilli strips to the broth and heat through.

8. Pour the warm broth into warm bowls and sprinkle diced avocado and coriander over it.

Serving: Serve the soup hot with the lemon wedges.

11. Walnut Soup

"This elegant soup with its delicious and delicate flavour is served on special occasions", say Monica Medina-Mora and Angeles Ayala in their book, 'Fresh Mexican'. Walnut soup is ideal for cold months and is excellent for strengthening the immune system. Walnuts have cholesterol-lowering source of omega-3 essential fatty acids. They are also a good source of vitamins A, B and C and minerals such as calcium, copper, iron and manganese.

You Require: **Cooking Time:** 45 minutes.

Tomatoes chopped	2 nos.	Chipotle chilli	2 nos.
Walnuts	250 gm	Or any other dry chilli (deseeded)	2 nos.
Cooking oil	1 tbsp	Onion chopped	1 small
Chicken stock	7 cups	Salt	to taste
Freshly ground pepper	to taste		
Parsley for garnishing			

Preparation and Cooking

1. Remove the stems of the chillies; slit and remove the seeds. For the milder sauce, remove all the veins too. Put in a heavy-based frying pan over a medium heat and lightly roast the chillies for a few seconds on both the sides. Soak in 1 cup boiling water for 15 to 20 minutes.
2. Grind the walnuts saving a few for garnishing. Chop the saved walnuts and keep aside.
3. Heat oil in a large saucepan and sauté onion in it. Add garlic and stir for a few seconds. Now add tomatoes and cook for a few minutes. Keep stirring.
4. Add soaked chillies with water to the tomato mixture and blend to a smooth paste. Add some stock and pass through a sieve. Mix it with rest of the stock in a saucepan and gently simmer for 15 minutes or till cooked.
5. Blend the ground walnuts with rest of the stock until smooth; add to the tomato mixture and mix well; bring it to the boiling point and reduce the heat; simmer for 10 to 15 minutes; season well and check the taste.

Serving: Serve the soup in individual bowls and garnish it with chopped parsley and walnuts.

Tips: Chipotle chillies are jalapeno that are left on the vine until ripened and then dried and smoked. In addition to intense heat, they add wonderful smoky flavour to many dishes. Generally, chillies are turned into a puree and then used to season the dishes.

12. Corn Dumplings in Soup

Dumpling is a ball of steamed and seasoned dough often served in soup or with stewed meat. Dough can be prepared with all-purpose flour or combination of flours, corn, potato, cheese or meats. Other vegetables can also be added to the dough and then seasoned according to the taste. Since corn is a staple of Mexico, corn meal and corn kernel dumplings are fondly enjoyed with soups/stews.

You Require: **Cooking Time:** 30 minutes

Yellow corn meal	1 cup	Corn kernels cream style	½ cup
Flour	1cup	Or grated corn on cob	½ cup
Chopped onion	1 tbsp	Melted butter	2 tbsp
Egg	1 no.	Baking powder	2 and ½ tsp
Salt	2 tsp	Pepper	½ tsp
Fresh basil chopped	2 tbsp	Boiling water	2 cup

Veg/non-veg well flavoured soup or stew, 5 to 6 cups

Preparation and Cooking:

1. Sift together corn meal and salt and slowly add to hot water, stirring constantly for 2 minutes or until thick.
2. Remove from heat and cool.
3. Sift together ¾ cup flour, baking powder and pepper powder. Add to corn meal and mix well.
4. Beat egg; and add to the mixture along with onion, grated corn, basil and butter. Mix well.
5. Shape the mixture into balls; roll in remaining flour and drop on hot soup/stew. Cover tightly and cook for 12 to 15 minutes without opening the lid. Or cook in a microwave for 8 minutes, covered.

Serving: Serve it hot garnished with chopped basil or coriander.

13. Shrimp Ball Soup

(Sopa de Albondigas)

This soup is a simple speciality of Mexico's western coast. This soup is substantial. It is a kind of dish that can be served before crispy tacos or enchiladas. In this part of the country, shrimps are so plentiful that the cooks use them to fill up soups, shred them as filling for tacos and grind them for balls or cakes etc.

You Require:			**Cooking Time:** 45 minutes.
For Balls:			
Shrimps cleaned and de-veined	1 cup	Onion chopped very fine	½ no small
Egg yolk	1 large	Flour	2 tbsp
Oregano dried	½ tsp	Salt	½ tsp
Tomato chopped	¼ th	Vegetable oil	1 tbsp
For Soup:			
Fish stock or veg-stock	5 to 6 cups	Onion finely sliced	1 no.
Or water + soup cube		Coriander chopped	¼ cup
Lime, quartered	1 to 2 nos.		
Poblano roasted, peeled, seeded and cut into strips			1 no.
Tomato roasted, peeled, cored and chopped			1 no.

Preparation and Cooking:

1. Chop shrimps very fine, either working with knife or by using food processor, until turned into coarse puree.
2. Place the shrimps in a mixing bowl; add the onion, tomato, egg yolk, flour, oregano and salt; mix thoroughly; cover and refrigerate until you are ready to finish the soup.
3. Make broth in a large pan. Heat oil in a large saucepan and fry onion in it until brown in colour. Add the chilli strips and tomatoes and cook for a while.
4. Add stock/broth or water and taste-maker cube; bring it to the boiling point; cover and simmer for 15 minutes over medium heat, so that the flavours blend well. Season it well with salt.
5. 15 minutes before serving, poach the shrimp balls in the gently simmering soup. Form small balls out of shrimp mixture or put the rounded teaspoons of shrimp mixture, simmer gently for 8 to 10 minutes and then remove from the fire.

Serving: Ladle the soup into bowls and sprinkle with chopped coriander. Serve the lime wedges on the sides.

14. Sopa de Tortilla

(Tortilla Soup with Fresh Cheese and Chilli)

This is essentially a soup that is more common in Central and Southern Mexico. It is composed of chicken broth, crisp strips of tortillas, fresh cheese and dried chillies. Traditionally, Mexicans prefer goat cheese to fresh cheese, but simple cubed fresh cheese can do the needful.

You Require: **Cooking Time:** 1 hour.

Chicken broth	6 cups	Corn tortillas	4 to 6 nos.
Olive oil	2 tbsp	Onion sliced	1 no medium
Garlic peeled	2 cloves	Tomatoes roasted and peeled	2 nos.
Pasillas or any other dry chillies	2 nos.		
Cubed Mexican cheese		Fresh thyme	2 to 3 sprigs
or Other fresh cheese	2 cups		
Lime, cut into 6 pieces	1 large		
Salt	to taste	Freshly powdered pepper	½ tsp

Preparation and Cooking:

1. Heat 1 tbsp olive oil in a small pan on medium fire and add sliced onion and whole garlic cloves; fry until both are deep golden brown in colour and switch off the fire. Place them in a blender jar, add tomato and blend until smooth.
2. Heat the remaining oil in a deep pan, add the tomato mixture and stir constantly until thicker and darker in colour.
3. Stir in the broth, add fresh thyme, mix well and simmer for 30 minutes. Season it with salt and pepper. Remove the thyme sprigs before serving.
4. Cut tortillas into strips and fry till crisp. Or brush tortillas with oil, cut them into strips and bake in hot oven for 15 to 20 minutes or till crisp.
5. Cut the chillies into 1-inch pieces and just fry in hot oil for a while and remove immediately. Drain on paper towel.
6. Assemble the soup just before serving.

Serving: Divide the cheese among 4 to 6 soup bowls and top with fried tortilla strips. Pour the hot soup over, sprinkle thyme (if fresh one is not used); and serve it immediately. Pass the toasted chillies separately along with lime pieces. Squeeze lime into the soup for enriching the flavour.

Variations: Use well-flavoured vegetable stock and make soup the same way with cheese and serve it as a starter.

Add stewed and shredded chicken to the soup and serve it as a hearty main course.

Tips: Broth can be made and stored under refrigeration well in advance.

Instead of pasilla chilli, use any other dried chilli for frying and crumbling over the soup but do not use chilli powder.

15. Roasted Corn and Cilantro Soup

This is a nice soup of roasted corn and coriander which makes a light meal when served with any of the starters included in the the starters' section.

You Require: **Cooking Time:** 45 minutes to 1 hour.

Corn on the cobs	3 nos.	Green pepper	1 no.
Vegetable stock	6 cups	Veg. soup cube	1 no.
Onion, chopped fine	1 no.	Garlic, chopped fine	1 tbsp
Maize flour	1 tbsp	Olive oil	2 tbsp
Lemon juice	1 tbsp	Salt	to taste
Cilantro/coriander chopped	¼ cup	Green chilli, roasted and chopped	1 no.

Preparation and Cooking:

1. Roast green pepper on open fire till blackened from all sides and place it in a plastic bag for 20 minutes. Meantime, roast the corn on the cobs one by one and remove the niblets with a sharp fruit knife. Remove the green pepper from the bag and clean it with the blunt side of a knife. Chop it fine and keep aside.
2. Heat oil in a large pan on medium heat and fry chopped onion and garlic till pinkish in colour; add chopped pepper and green chilli; stir for a minute; add maize flour and cook for a few seconds.
3. Pour the stock into it and bring it to the boiling point. Add roasted corn niblets and simmer for 15 minutes.
4. Remove from the fire and add lemon juice and chopped coriander/cilantro.

Serving: Serve it immediately with 'Prawns on Skewers' or any other starter.

Blackbeans Soup

Ensaladas/Salads

Apple and Walnut Salad, 76

Avocado Salad, 75

Broccoli Salad, 77

Butter Bean Salad with Toasted Almond Flakes, 74

Chicken Salad with Jalapeno Dressing, 79

Chicken-n-fruit Salad with Lemon-Honey Dressing, 80

Corn and Pineapple Salad, 75

Mexican Vegetable Salad, 73

Mushroom and Spinach Salad, 76

Spicy Turnip-Radish Salad, 82

Sautéd Prawns/Shrimps' Salad, 81

Orange and Raisins Salad, 78

Watermelon and Roasted Corn Salad, 79

Ensaladas/Salads

Health-conscious Mexicans eat salad, one for lunch and one for supper. But most Mexicans have their salads sprinkled on their tacos or other snacks. The fact remains that they eat a fair amount of salad everyday. Their salads include meats, poultry, fish/ seafood, vegetables, fruits and nuts. Of course, different dressings are prepared to season and flavour the salads. They are served as appetizers as well as light main course.

1. Mexican Vegetable Salad

(Ensalada Mixta)

You Require: **Preparation Time:** 20 minutes.

Ripe tomatoes	2 nos.	Cucumber	1 no medium
Onions	2 nos.	Fresh mushroom	8 nos.
Red bell pepper	1 no. small	Green pepper	1 no small
Yellow pepper	1 no. small	Black and green olives	10 nos.
Carrot	1 no. medium	Celery stick	1 no.
Jalapeno chopped	1 no. (opt)	Table radish	3 nos.

Seasonings:

Lime	1 no.	Olive oil	1 to 2 tbsp
Tabasco/hot sauce	1 tbsp	Salt-n-pepper	to taste
Lettuce	6 leaves		

Preparation:

1. Slice tomatoes, radish and mushrooms; dice cucumber and onions and cut bell peppers and carrot into juliennes.
2. Chop celery fine.
3. Deseed jalapeno and chop very fine.
4. Cut olives into rings.
5. Wash and break lettuce into pieces.
6. Squeeze the lime and mix with tabasco, olive oil, salt and freshly crushed pepper. Mix it in a bottle and shake well.
7. Combine all the vegetables in a salad bowl; sprinkle seasonings over the vegetables and toss the salad.

Serving: Arrange the salad on a bed of lettuce artistically. Serve it with grilled or roasted chicken or with any other Mexican meal.

Variation: You can have different combination of vegetables, for example, boiled and sliced potatoes, par-boiled green beans, sliced radishes, peeled and sliced cucumber and cored and sliced tomatoes, etc.

Lime dressing: Combine 3 tbsp freshly squeezed lime juice, ½ cup vegetable and olive oil mixed, ½ tsp salt, a generous/big pinch of freshly ground black pepper and 2 tbsp chopped coriander or parsley. Mix all the ingredients a few minutes before serving in a jar or a bottle with a tight-fitting lid and shake well until thoroughly blended. Pour over vegetables and mix well.

Note: The preparation time depends on the number of vegetables you choose. Par-boiled vegetables (wherever required) or steamed vegetables can be prepared, covered and stored under refrigeration beforehand (a day ahead) and raw vegetables several hours before but the dressing should be added just before serving, so that the vegetables don't lose the crispness.

2. Butter Bean Salad with Toasted Almond Flakes

You Require: **Cooking Times:** 10 minutes.

Butter beans	500 gm	Shallots	20 nos.
Cucumber	1 no.	Cherry tomatoes	20 nos.
Olives (black) sliced	10 nos.		
Seasonings:			
Lemon juice	2 tbsp	Freshly crushed pepper	1 tsp
Olive oil	2 tbsp	Almond flakes	¼ cup
Pizza chilli flakes	1 tsp (opt)	Salt	to taste

Preparation and Cooking:

1. Wash, string and cut beans into 1-inch long pieces. Place them in the steaming basket of your microwave and steam for 5 minutes on HIGH; stand for 2 minutes and run under cold water.
2. Or boil the beans in minimum water and run under cold water.
3. Cut cucumber into bite sized pieces.
4. Halve the cherry tomatoes. Clean the shallots.
5. Combine beans, tomatoes, shallots, olives, lemon juice, salt and pepper. Toss well.
6. Heat oil in a pan and switch off the heat; fry almond flakes to golden and pour over the tossed salad. Toss it once again.

Serving: Garnish the beans salad with chilli flakes and serve with Tortillas/Enchiladas or roasted meats.

Tips: You may buy the fresh bean bag ready to be cooked in the microwave and follow the instructions.

After steaming green vegetables, such as beans, broccoli, green peas or spinach if run under cold water, they retain their green colour.

3. Avocado Salad

Avocado salad is one of the Mexican specialties which is prepared all over the country and served with various snacks as an accompaniment or with meals as a side dish.

You Require: **Preparation Time:** 15 minutes.

Ripe Avocado	1 no.	Chopped onion	1 tbsp
Jalapeno chilli	1 no.	Coriander chopped	1 tbsp
Lemon juice	1 tsp	Salt	to taste

Preparation:

1. Halve the avocado, remove and discard the stone; cut the avocado flesh into small pieces.
2. Mix chopped onion, coriander and chilli with avocado, sprinkle lemon juice over it and season it with salt.

   Serving: Garnish it with extra chopped coriander and serve with crisp tortilla chips.

4. Corn and Pineapple Salad

This simple tangy-refreshing salad makes an excellent light meal, when accompanied with fish steak.

You Require: **Preparation Time:** 35 minutes.

Fresh pineapple	1 no.	Corn kernels steamed	1 and ½ cup
Chilli flakes	1 to 2 tsp	Chopped mint	3 tbsp
Green chilli	2 nos.	Cucumber unpeeled	1 medium
Capsicum juliennes	¼ cup	Lettuce	8 to 10 leaves
Seasonings:			
Lime juice	1 tbsp	Olive oil	1 tbsp
Salt-n-pepper	to taste		

Preparation:

1. Cut cucumber into roundels or squares, and green chillies into small pieces.
2. Clean and cut pineapple into chunks.
3. Immerse lettuce in cold water.
4. Mix together lime juice, olive oil, salt and pepper.
5. Combine corn, pineapple, cucumber, capsicum and green chillies in a bowl and toss. Add seasonings and mix with a light hand. Chill for 30 minutes.
6. Remove lettuce from water and shake well to remove extra water. You may line a platter with it or break the leaves in edible size and mix with the rest of the salad ingredients.
7. Add mint leaves before serving.

Serving: Pile up salad in the centre of the serving plate and sprinkle red chilli flakes over it. Serve the salad chilled.

5. Mushroom and Spinach Salad

This simply elegant salad is very refreshing and is an excellent accompaniment to any dish of grilled fish or roasted meats. It goes well with egg preparation too.

You Require: **Preparation Time:** 15 to 20 minutes.

Mushrooms	200 gm	Spinach	30 leaves
Olive oil	2 tbsp	(Baby spinach preferable)	
Sesame seeds	1 tbsp	Salt	1 tsp
Lemon juice	2 tsp (opt)	Freshly crushed pepper	1 tsp

Preparation:

1. Heat a non-stick pan or a griddle and roast sesame seeds till their flavour is enhanced.
2. Or roast ½ cup sesame seeds in a microwave. Place them in a paper bag and roast on micro HIGH for 2 minutes, shaking the envelope once in between after 1 minute. Cool and store. If the quantity is more than required, use as much as required and store the rest in a glass container for further use.
3. Wash and dry spinach gently.
4. Clean and wipe the mushrooms with a kitchen napkin and slice.
5. Arrange the spinach and mushroom in a serving dish; pour oil all over and season with salt and freshly crushed peppercorns.

Serving: Sprinkle sesame seeds on top of the salad evenly and serve it immediately.

6. Apple and Walnut Salad

In Mexico, it is a tradition to serve this delicious salad at the Christmas time, as it is an ideal accompaniment to roasted turkey. It is not only nutritious but also cleansing as apples are a good source of fiber and vitamins A and C; and walnuts are a good source of protein, iron and calcium.

You Require: **Preparation Time:** 20 minutes.

Apples	3 nos.	Pineapple slices	4 nos.
Lemon	1 no.	Walnuts chopped	1/3 cup
Celery sticks chopped fine	2 nos.	Mayonnaise sauce	2 tbsp
Salt	to taste	Freshly crushed pepper	to taste
Salad leaves	6 to 8 nos.		

Preparation:

1. Wash and core the apples. Peel the two of them and dice. Dice the one without peeling for the tinge of red. Combine and squeeze lemon juice over them to avoid discolouration.
2. Dice the pineapple too in ½ inch pieces.
3. Combine the fruits and walnuts in a bowl.
4. Add mayonnaise and mix it thoroughly. Stir in salt and pepper for seasoning and refrigerate for 30 minutes.

Serving: Garnish the salad with additional apple slices and serve in a platter lined with salad leaves immediately.

7. Broccoli Salad

One of the most colourful salads, not only that accompanies very well with all the appetizers but also provides an aesthetic feast.

You Require: **Preparation Time:** 35 minutes.

Broccoli	1 head of medium size	Tomato	1 no.
Apple	1 no.	Peppers red, green or yellow	½ each
Onion cut into rings	1 no.	Salad leaves	6 to 8 leaves
Freshly crushed peppercorns 1 tsp or to taste			
Lemon juice	1 tbsp	Salt	1 tsp or to taste
Tomato juice	¼ cup	Sugar	1 tsp
Garlic crushed	1 tsp	Coriander chopped	¼ cup (opt)
Rock salt	to taste		

Preparation and Cooking:

1. Combine together lemon juice, soy sauce, tomato juice, salt, pepper and garlic for dressing; mix well and chill.
2. Immerse salad leaves in cold water.
3. Break broccoli into small flowerets; wash and place in the steaming basket of a microwave and steam for 2 minutes on HIGH; remove, drain and rinse under the tap water to maintain its colour and crunchiness. Cool. Place in a salad bowl.
4. Dice apple without peeling into ½-inch pieces and sprinkle sugar over it to avoid discolouration. Toss.
5. Deseed tomato and cut into ½-inch squares.
6. Deseed and cut peppers too into the same size pieces.
7. Combine vegetables and fruit together, and toss.
8. Pour the chilled dressing over; sprinkle coriander; mix lightly with a fork and chill for 30 minutes at least.
9. Remove the salad leaves from water and keep under refrigeration.

Serving: Line a platter or another shallow dish with salad leaves and pile up the broccoli salad in the centre. Sprinkle some more pepper on top. Serve the salad with lemon wedges.

Tips: In the absence of broccoli, use cauliflower for this preparation.

8. Orange and Raisins Salad

This soft and crunchy salad, flavoured with lemon and pepper is excellent for hot summer months.

You Require: **Preparation Time:** 35 minutes.

Oranges	6 to 8 nos.	Raisins	1/3 cup
Grapes	1 cup	Cabbage shredded fine	2 to 3 cup
Candid orange peel	2 tbsp	Lemon	1 no.
For dressing:			
Mayonnaise	½ cup	Cream	½ cup
Mustard powder	½ tsp	Fresh crushed pepper	2 tsp leveled
Salt	to taste	Lettuce leaves to serve on	6 to 8 nos.

Preparation:

1. Wash and dip salad leaves in cold water.
2. Wash and drain cabbage.
3. Clean and soak raisins in lukewarm water for 15 to 20 minutes.
4. Peel oranges and take out the piths.
5. Clean, wash and halve the grapes.
6. Cut candid orange peel in thin strips.
7. Mix together cabbage, orange segments and grapes in a bowl; squeeze lemon over it; sprinkle 1 tsp salt and toss. Chill for 30 minutes.
8. Combine mayonnaise, cream, mustard powder, salt and pepper.

Assembling: Take out the salad leaves from water and shake them well. Arrange them in a platter. Mix chilled fruits and vegetables with the mayonnaise dressing and soaked raisins and pile up in the platter. Garnish with additional orange segments and chopped candid peels.

Serving: Serve this soothing salad as a starter or as an accompaniment or part of any Mexican meal.

Variation: This fruity salad goes very well with chilli croutons or plain croutons, as soft fruits taste excellent with crunchy croutons.

Tips: Instead of using lemon and pepper powder separately, you can use lemon pepper to flavour the salad.

Fruits and cabbage can be prepared and chilled in advance and mixing can be done before serving.

9. Watermelon and Roasted Corn Salad

An unusual combination of popular ingredients makes a very refreshing and satisfying salad.

You Require: **Preparation Time:** 35 to 40 minutes.

Watermelon	1 no medium	Capsicum green	1 no. small
Corn kernels	1 and ½ cup	Green chillies	2 nos.
Or corn on cobs	2 nos. large	Lemon juice	from 1 lemon
Sugar	½ tsp	Pepper powder	½ tsp
Salt	1 tsp	Coriander chopped	¼ cup
Cottage cheese crumbled	¼ cup	Olive oil	2 tbsp (opt)

Preparation and Cooking:

1. Cut watermelon into halves; cut into cubes or take out the balls. Chill.
2. Roast corn kernels on a hot griddle or in a kadai and keep aside. If you are using corn on cobs, roast them directly on the flames of a naked fire till brownish black. Remove the corn from the cobs with the help of a knife.
3. Deseed the green chillies and capsicum and cut into small pieces.
4. Mix lemon juice, salt, pepper and olive oil together for the dressing.
5. Combine watermelon, corn, capsicum and green chillies in a serving bowl; add half the coriander; pour over the dressing and toss well. Chill.

Serving: Garnish the salad with the remaining coriander and crumbled cottage cheese. Serve as a starter in individual bowls or in a platter with a meal.

Tips: In the absence of fresh corn, frozen American corn kernels can be used.

10. Chicken Salad with Jalapeno Dressing

You Require: **Cooking Time:** 25 to 30 minutes.

Cooked and shredded chicken	3 cups	Olive oil	2 tbsp
Or leftovers from roasted chicken		Jalapenos/green chillies	2 nos.
Shallots	12 to 15 nos.	Cherry tomatoes	12 to 16 nos.
Garlic chopped fine	4 cloves	Or tomatoes	2 nos. medium
Thyme dried	½ tsp	Celery sticks	2 nos.
Carrot	1 no. (opt)	Apples	2 nos.
Lemon	1 no.	Almonds blanched	½ cup
Raisins (golden)	¼ cup		

Dressing:

Jalapeno dressing	1 recipe

Preparation and Cooking:

1. Chop chillies and celery very fine.
2. Halve the cherry tomatoes or deseed tomato and cut into strips.
3. Peel and shred carrot.
4. Clean shallots and keep aside.
5. Toast blanched almonds and slice.
6. Combine cherry tomatoes, celery, carrot and raisins in a bowl and mix the dressing.
7. Core and cut apples into halves and then slice and toss them too with the dressing to avoid discolouration.
8. Heat the olive oil in a large pan or kadai and put jalapenos and onions; stir till onions are slightly transparent but still crisp. Add the garlic and cook for one minute. Add shredded chicken and thyme and cook gently till chicken absorbs seasoning. Chicken may stick to the bottom of the pan but separate the pieces.
9. Now mix chicken with the other ingredients tossed with dressing. Toss it or mix with a fork gently.

Serving: Garnish with almonds and additional cherry tomatoes and serve. Serve the salad in individual plates or bowls if serving as a starter.

Tips: Warming the chicken with onions and herbs, adds flavour to the salad.

11. Chicken-n-Fruit Salad with Lemon-Honey Dressing

This full-of-protein salad is predominantly sweet and sour in flavour and is ideal for those salad lovers who prefer to have just large salad at lunch.

You Require: **Cooking Time:** 10 to 15 minutes for cooking chicken breasts and 15 minutes for mixing and presentation.

Chicken breasts	2 to 3 nos.	Adobo sauce	1 tbsp
Honey	1 tbsp	Lemon juice	3 to 4 tbsp
Mango	1 large	Pineapple pieces	2 cups
Cucumbers	2 small	Red pepper	1 medium
Celery	2 sticks	Jalapeno chilli	1 no.
Lemon-honey dressing	1 recipe (chilled)		
Chilli croutons	2 cups (opt)	Salt	½ tsp if required
Salad leaves	1 head		

Preparation and Cooking:

1. Prepare a marinade by mixing together honey, lemon juice, adobo and salt.

2. Wash and dry chicken breasts with kitchen towels; pound them with a mallet/meat flattener to ½-inch thickness and rub them nicely with marinade made of honey, lemon, adobo and salt.
3. Cover and refrigerate for 1 day, turning them once in between or for 2 hours at room temperature.
4. Heat a gas grill to medium heat or prepare a charcoal grill.
5. Remove the chicken breasts from the marinade and cook under the grill for about 10 minutes, turning them once in between. Grill it till cooked through and charred in places.
6. Remove the chicken to the chopping board; cover with foil and let it stand for 5 minutes to retain the moisture. Then cut it into ½ inch pieces and keep aside, covered.
7. Peel the mango, pit it and cut it into ½ inch cubes.
8. Peel and cut cucumbers, cut red pepper into small pieces and chop celery and jalapeno.
9. Place cut fruits, vegetables, meat pieces and croutons in a large bowl; pour over chilled lemon-honey dressing and mix it lightly with salad spoons.

Serving: Line a salad bowl or a platter with salad leaves and pile up the salad in the centre and serve it part of the main course.

Or serve it in individual plates as a starter.

Tips: This is a vendor style salad sold in Mexico city. There the vendors sell all type of fruits cut into cubes or strips and season the salad with lime, salt and chilli and serve in paper cups. Added chicken to fruits makes the dish special and worth serving it as a main course dish.

12. Sautéd Prawns/Shrimps' Salad

You Require: **Cooking Time:** 30 to 40 minutes.

Prawns cleaned and de-veined	16 to 20 nos.	Lime-cilantro dressing	1/4 to 1/2 cup
Or cleaned shrimps	300 gm	Lemon juice	3 tbsp
Pepper powder	½ tsp	Salt	to taste (opt)
Olive oil	2 tbsp	White onion	2 noS.
Red pepper	½ no.	Green/yellow pepper	½ no.
Lettuce head	1 small		

Preparation and Cooking:

1. Wash and marinate cleaned prawns or shrimps with lemon juice and pepper for 20 to 30 minutes.
2. Meantime clean and cut onions and red and yellow peppers into rings.
3. Soak lettuce in cold water for 20 minutes; break or chop roughly into pieces and keep under refrigeration.

4. Drain prawns and discard juices (with raw smell).
5. Heat oil in a pan and sauté prawns in it for 7 to 8 minutes on high fire. Remove.
6. Combine all the chopped ingredients in a bowl; place prawns on top and pour dressing over it.
7. Line a serving plate with lettuce.

Serving: Mix the salad lightly with a fork and serve on lettuce with any meal.

13. Spicy Turnip-Radish Salad

You Require: **Preparation Time:** 45 minutes.

Small turnips	2 to 3 nos.	White radish	1 no.
Orange juice (unsweetened)	½ cup	Salt	¼ tsp
Red skinned apple	1 no.	Cucumber	1 no.
Orange	1 no.	Olive oil	1 tsp
Or tangerines	3 nos.	Apple	1 no (opt)
Coriander chopped	2 tbsp		
Chilli powder	1 tsp	Lettuce	4 leaves

Preparation:

1. Clean and cut turnip and radish, either into ½-inch cube or matchstick fashion; place them into a glass bowl, pour orange juice and sprinkle with salt. Toss well, cover and let stand at room temperature for half-an-hour or so.
2. Clean orange or tangerine segments, seed and break into pieces.
3. Cut apple and cucumber also into ½-cubes.
4. Soak lettuce in cold water for 15 to 30 minutes, drain, shake extra water and break into pieces. Keep under refrigeration till in use.
5. 15 to 20 minutes before serving add the apple, cucumber, orange/tangerines, oil and coriander to the bowl of turnip and radish and mix thoroughly.
6. Toss the mixture every 5 minutes until time to serve. Season it with chilli powder. Check if more salt is required.

Serving: Place lettuce in a serving bowl and pile up the salad on top. Sprinkle with 1 pinch chilli powder and 1 tbsp fresh coriander once again.

Variation: Use Jicama, a variety of beetroot, white in colour, instead of turnip and radish and follow the rest of the recipe.

Bebidas/Spiritz/Mocktails and Refreshing Drinks

Agua de Tamarindo, 89

Agua de Hibiscus, 88

Hot Chocolate Beverage, 90

Hot Punch, 92

Mango Torito, 86

Margarita, 86

Melon and Water-melon Coolers, 85

Lemonade, 87

Quick Fruit and Milk Smoothy, 90

Orange Sensation, 84

Sensational Grapes and Raspberries Refresher, 85

Sangrita, 84

Bebidas/Spiritz/Mocktails and Refreshing Drinks

Mexican cuisine is inseparable from the drinks that accompany it. They are delicious and unusual and they give the Mexican meals an authentic flavour. That is why, after a hectic day, the Mexicans refresh themselves with chilled fruit and vegetable drinks. In some, even Tequila is added for that extra zest. Tequila and Bloody Mary, the popular drinks originate from Mexico. Between the Tequila shots sips of fruits- and vegetables-based refreshers are enjoyed.

A few words about the famous Tequila:

Tequila is produced from the heart of blue agave plant, which thrives in the dry volcanic soil in the state of Jalisco and many other parts of Mexico. The hearts of this plant are roasted, releasing a sweet sap, that is then distilled. The liquor that results, can be called tequila, only if it is produced in Jalisco – where the town of Tequila is one of the two main centers of production, or in other 4 government-approved regions. Any similar liquor produced elsewhere in Mexico is called **mezcal or stool**.

There are 2 basic types of tequila: 100% agave and mixto. Only tequila made from the sap of the agave plant can be labeled "100%"; mixtos can be made with the addition of other alcohols, such as rum and syrups.

Within the tequila family, there are 4 subcategories:

Silver tequila: Silver tequila or blanco, as it is known in Mexico, is clear and mild and has not been aged. These tequilas are used primarily in margaritas and other mixed drinks, not drunk on their own.

Gold tequila: Gold tequila is nothing else but silver tequila that has been coloured and flavoured with caramel or another flavour.

Reposado: (rested) Tequila must, by law, be aged in wooden casks for a minimum of 60 days.

Anejo: (aged) Tequila is aged in wooden barrels for a minimum of 12 months. "The best quality anejos are aged from 18 months to 3 years", says Roberto Santibanez, chef, Rosa Mexicana.

1. Orange and Tomato Sensation

This twin-flavoured fruit sensation is not only very refreshing but healthy too. It stimulates appetite and wards off constipation.

You Require: **Preparation Time:** 15 minutes.

Preserved tomato juice	3 cups	Preserved orange juice	3 cups
Salt	½ tsp	Pepper powder	½ tsp
Mint chopped	2 tbsp	Orange	1 no.
Ice cubes	1 cup	Sugar	2 tbsp (opt)

Preparation:

1. Wash and cut orange into thin slices without peeling.
2. Combine the juices, salt, pepper, ice cubes, half the mint, half the orange with peels and sugar in a blender. Churn it for a while and strain through a sieve.
3. Add a few mint leaves in each glass and pour the juice over it.

Serving: Serve each glass of 'Orange and Tomato Sensation' garnished with orange slices as a starter.

Tips: When in season you may use fresh orange and tomato juice instead of ready-made preserved ones.

2. Sangrita

(Tomato-based Drink)

Though spicy-n-tasty Sangrita stimulates the senses, yet this is not regarded a beverage. "Sangrita is not a beverage, it is more of a condiment to be enjoyed when sipping Tequila, you taste a little tequila, then sip a little sangrita, and repeat", says Roberto Santibanez.

You Require: **Preparation Time:** 15 minutes, chilling time extra.

Tomatoes roasted, cooled and peeled 6 nos.			
Or readymade tomato juice	3 cup	Onion chopped fine	1 no.
Green chilli deseeded and chopped	1 no.	Orange juice	1 cup
Lemon juice from	1 lemon	Or lime juice	from half a lime
Salt	½ tsp	Sugar to taste or no sugar	

Preparation:

1. Combine all the ingredients in a blender and churn until the mixture is smooth.
2. Strain through a sieve and place under refrigeration at least for 30 minutes to 1 hour.
3. Do not keep in a refrigerator for more than 2 days, otherwise the onion flavour will dominate.

Serving: Serve Sangrita chilled.

Tips: There are many versions of making sangrita, but making with tomatoes or tomato juice is the most popular one.

3. Melon and Water-melon Coolers

In Mexico, all over the country, refreshing and delicious fruit coolers are sold, and melons are one of those fruits that are widely used. The seeds of the melons and water melons are also added while pureeing the fruits for cooling drinks and later strained. Such refreshing coolers not only quench the thirst in hot summer days but these highly nutritious drinks are also excellent cleansers and re-hydrators. They are a good source of potassium and vitamins, A and C.

You Require: **Preparation Time:** 15 minutes and chilling time extra.

Ripe melon	1 no.	Water	1000 ml
Or small watermelon	1 no.	Castor sugar	to taste
Ice cubes to serve with			

Preparation:

1. Peel the melons and roughly chop the melons' flesh into pieces; put in blender with the seeds and blend to a puree. And Pour measured water and strain the mixture through a sieve into a jug.
2. Add sugar and mix well; cover and chill in the refrigerator till required.

Serving: Pour melon water into glasses. Add some crushed ice and decorate with small melon cubes or balls. Serve chilled any time.

4. Sensational Grapes and Raspberries Refresher

You Require: **Preparation Time:** 15 minutes and chilling time extra.

Black grapes	2 cups	Raspberries	1 cup
Lemon	½ no.	Sugar	1 tbsp
Soda/aerated water Ice cubes	800 ml		

Preparation and cooking:

1. Mix together raspberries and sugar in a micro safe bowl, squeeze lemon over and cook for 3 minutes, covered. Cool.
2. Place grapes and raspberry mixture in a blender and blend well till smooth. Strain through a strainer. Chill the mixture.
3. Crush ice and put into 4 to 6 glasses.
4. Add aerated water/soda to the juice.
5. Pour juice mixture into the glasses and stir.

Serving: Serve it chilled with a stirrer in each glass.

5. Margarita

Whenever the Mexican food is on menu, the drink that comes to mind is Margarita. The sweet and sour pale green cocktail that is presented in salt and lime rimmed glasses, is actually linked to Mexico by its shot of tequila.

You Require: **Preparation Time:** 5 to 7 minutes.

Silver tequila	3 tbsp	Cointreau or Triple sec	1 and ½ tbsp
Fresh lime juice	1 and ½ tbsp	Superfine sugar	1 tbsp
Ice cubes	½ cup	Lime wedge	1 no.
Salt rimmed tall glass	1 no. (opt)		

Preparation:

1. **Prepare a salt rimmed glass.** Spread an even layer of sea salt on a plate; lightly rub the lime around the outside rim of the glass; lightly press the rim of the glass into the salt; lift the glass and shake excess (extra salt); and allow the salt to air dry before filling the glass, so that you can avoid too much salt coming off the glass with each sip.
2. Put 6 to 8 cubes in a tall cocktail or coffee shaker and shake vigorously. Pour ice and all other ingredients into the large glass.

Note: You can multiply the recipe according to your need.

Serving: Garnish the drink with a lime wedge and serve in a salt rimmed glass.

Tips: Mexicans serve a variety of margaritas, made with passion fruit and other ones.

Information: The custom of salt with margaritas, perhaps, has something to do with hot and humid climate of Mexico as Mexico, by and large, is a hot and semi-tropical country. In Mexico salt is used liberally in order to restore what is lost during the day through perspiration. Salt helps absorb and retain water in the body more quickly. Many a margarita drinkers prefer to sip the drink from plain glasses rather than from salt-rimmed glasses.

6. Mango Torito

Toritos are brightly coloured and refreshing fruit based drinks that are served as aperitifs (a small drink of alcoholic liquor taken before a meal to stimulate the appetite).

You Require: **Preparation Time:** 30 minutes.

Large ripe mango	1 no	Water	2 cups
Or Mango puree	1 cup	Super-fine sugar	1 cup
Silver tequila	1 cup	Fresh squeezed lime juice	½ cup

Preparation:

1. Remove the flesh from the mango, thoroughly, cut it into pieces and puree.

2. Fill a jug or any other pitcher with ice and pour in the mango puree, water, sugar, lime-juice and tequila.
3. Stir the mixture until the sugar is dissolved completely.

Serving: Serve Mango torito on ice before a meal.

7. Limeade/Limonada/Lemonade

Since lime is one of Mexico's national flavours and a glass of cold sweet-sour limeade is one of the national drinks. It is commonly prepared because this non-alcoholic drink nicely compliments Mexican meals. Not only this refresher is easy to prepare at home and is the choice of majority, but also is easily available in coffee shops and restaurants.

You Require: **Preparation time:** 30 minutes or so.

Sugar	1/2 to 2/3 cup	Fresh lime juice (from 8 to 10 limes)	1 and 1/3 cup
Water boiled and cooled	5 to 6 cups		
Ice cubes	1 cup or more		

Preparation:

1. First add ½ cup sugar to lime juice and stir till dissolved.
2. Add water and mix properly; taste the sweetness desired and add more sugar if required.

Serving: Place 4 to 5 ice cubes in each glass and pour the mixture over ice. Serve it immediately.

Variation: Make the Limeade and then stir in ½ to ¾ cup Vodka or Sugar-cane alcohol. It will be called **Veracruz style Torito.**

8. Horchata

(Almond-Rice Cooler)

Horchata, a light and rich drink is one of the popular refreshing drinks made in Mexico, by steeping nuts and grains. It is an ancient drink that is introduced to Mexico by the Spanish. This version is made with ground rice and almonds, spiced with cinnamon and sweetened with sugar. It is a healthy drink as it is a good source of protein and an excellent food for those who are underweight.

You Require: **Preparation time:** 8 to 10 hours.

Long grained rice	½ cup	Almonds (ground)	1 cup
Cinnamon	1 stick of 1 inch piece	Sugar	1 cup

Three strips of 2-inch long and ½-inch wide lime zest (rind)

Water	2 and ½ cup	Cinnamon powder	1 tsp to serve with
Semi skimmed milk/water	3 cups		

Preparation:

1. Clean, rinse and soak rice in 2 and ½ cups of water.
2. Crumble cinnamon, roast it lightly in a small pan and add it to the soaking rice. Add lime zest also to the rice and let rice stand overnight.
3. First blend rice in a blender with 1 cup water; add remaining water, almonds, cinnamon stick and lime zest and again blend for 3 to 4 minutes.
4. Place a large sieve on a bowl lined with 2 layers of cheese cloth. Pour in the rice-almond mixture and stir gently to help the liquid pass through. Strain it in 2 batches.
5. When all the liquid has been strained, gather up the corners of the cheese cloth and twist them together firmly to squeeze the remaining liquid.
6. Add milk and sugar and stir. If the consistency of the mixture seems thick, add additional water. Cover and refrigerate until required. Chill thoroughly before serving.

Serving: Stir the drink just before serving. Pour it into the glasses, add ice cubes and dust the top of horchata with cinnamon powder.

Tips: How to take out lime zest? With a sharp fruit knife tàke out the peel from the lime and cut into desired sized pieces.

9. Agua de Hibiscus

(Hibiscus Flower Cooler)

Dried hibiscus flowers are widely used in Mexico for making bright coloured, flavourful refreshing drink all over the country. This refreshing beverage is one of the most popular ones as it has health value too. Hibiscus, not only contains antioxidants that help control cholesterol level and reduce heart disease, but also it has diuretic property and mild blood vessel dilating effects.

You Require: **Cooking Time:** 45 minutes.

Hibiscus flowers dried	50 gm	Castor sugar	50 gm or to taste
Water	6 cups	Ice cubes	to serve with

Preparation and Cooking:

1. Put 4 cups of water and hibiscus flowers in a pan over medium heat and bring to the boiling point; reduce the heat and simmer for 15 minutes.
2. Remove from fire and leave to infuse for 30 minutes.
3. Strain the liquid through a fine mesh in a vessel and add sugar. Stir until the sugar is fully dissolved. Strain once again through the mesh lined with a single layer of cheese cloth, if you find some sediments settled at bottom of the vessel.

4. Add the remaining water and cool it thoroughly. Cover and refrigerate till required.

Serving: Serve with crushed ice or ice cubes.

Tips: This cold beverage can be prepared one day in advance and stored under refrigeration.

10. Agua de Tamarindo

(Tamarind Cooler)

In the hot humid climate delicious tamarind coolers prepared with tamarind pod or pulp are very refreshing and soothing. Ice cold 'tamarindo' is delicious with grilled food as well as with tacos and enchiladas etc.

You Require: **Cooking Time:** Approximately 2 and ½ hours, if pods are used. 30 minutes if tamarind pulp is used. Chilling time extra.

Tamarind pods	10 large	Sugar	¾ cup or to taste
Or tamarind paste	½ cup	Water	5 to 6 cups

Preparation:

1. Clean the tamarind pods. Hold a pod in the hand, pull out the stem and peel off the shells.
2. Boil 3 cups of water in a stainless steel or glass vessel; add the tamarind pods and sugar, and boil for 5 minutes. Let the mixture stand for 2 hours.
3. Mash the pods either with your hand or with wooden spoon to separate the seeds and the pulp.
4. Strain the mixture through a fine sieve, pressing hard with the back of a spoon to extract as much liquid (essence) as possible.
5. Or place the tamarind pulp in a blender jar, add 2 cups of boiled and cooled water and sugar, and pulse in on and off manner until the seeds are dislodged (separated). Add remaining water and churn once more. Strain and extract as much liquid as possible.
6. Check the sweetness to suit your taste; cover and refrigerate till required. Stir before serving.

Serving: Serve chilled tamarindo in clear glasses.

Variation: Contemporary ideas: prepare tamarindo as directed; stir in ½ cup brandy and ¼ cup fresh lemon juice.

Information: Spanish call such drinks **'agua frescas'**, which literally means "fresh waters". They are referred to as 'agues preparadas' (prepared waters), to emphasize that they are made rather than bought from the stores (ready-mades) like soda pop etc.

11. Quick Fruit and Milk Smoothy

(Licuado de Lechey Fruta)

Fruit smoothies or 'licuados' as the Mexicans call them, are one of the varieties of Mexican refreshment. These quick drinks that are at their best when served immediately (shortly after blending), are not only delicious and nutritive but also healthy. That is why, the entire nation enjoys these blender-made concoctions enthusiastically. Since they are made with milk, they are filling and form a complete breakfast.

You Require: **Preparation Time:** 10 minutes.

Cold milk	1 cup	Sugar	1 to 1 and ½ tbsp
Any fruit	½ to ¾ cup		

Banana, mango, papaya, strawberry, cantaloupe, watermelon, persimmon and guava, etc., (peeled, hulled, seeded, cored as necessary) cut into small pieces

Preparation:

1. Combine all the ingredients in an electric blender and blend until very smooth.
2. Strain the mixture, if there are any seeds or fibers.

Note: This quantity of ingredients will yield 1 large glass of fruit and milk beverage to you. You may multiply or double the recipe according to your own requirement.

Serving: Serve in large glasses.

Variation: Many people prefer to make smoothies with water instead of milk and add less fruit and more sugar. Some fruits like watermelon and pineapple taste better that way. Some also add a little chopped fruit as garnishing.

12. Hot Chocolate Beverage

"Coco/cacao is one of the most important Mexican contributions to the gastronomic world. Chocolate is a pre-Hispanic ritual beverage, made with cacao and water and served cold with plenty of foam. The present practice of using milk or cream and serving it hot is widely accepted. One of the most popular chocolate bars used to prepare this drink contains ground coco, sugar, cinnamon, almond and vanilla".

You Require: **Cooking Time:** 10 to 15 minutes.

Semi-skimmed milk or water	1000 ml	Plain dark chocolate chopped	200 gm
Cinnamon powder	a pinch (opt)	Powdered sugar	1 tbsp (opt)

Preparation and Cooking:

1. Place chopped chocolate and 1 cup milk or water in a pan over a medium heat; bring the mixture to the boiling point and remove from the heat.

2. Heat remaining milk on low fire/heat.
3. With a whisk or a rotary beater, beat the chocolate mixture vigorously until the chocolate is completely melted and the mixture is thick and foamy.
4. Gradually, pour in the remaining hot milk; warm over gentle heat, whisking all the time to make the beverage foamy.

Serving: Pour the hot chocolate in individual cups and serve immediately.

Variation: Iced Chocolate: Reduce the quantity of chocolate in the recipe to 150 gm and prepare foamy chocolate. Add 3 to 4 tbsp castor sugar. Let the mixture cool completely, preferably overnight under refrigeration. Now place it in a blender, add a few ice cubes, churn it for a while and serve it immediately.

They say that by keeping prepared chocolate overnight under refrigeration, it improves the flavour of the drink, gives it special smoothness and makes it frothy.

Information: Though chocolate was discovered in Mexico, later Spanish introduced it into Europe. The Jesuits were the first to improve this exotic product. Chocolate at this time was always prepared with water. It was very sweet and was flavoured with vanilla. It was Austria, Spain and France where chocolate was mostly consumed in liquid form.

In spite of their fat content, cocoa beans are rather nutritious. They supply useful amounts of proteins, some B vitamins and trace elements, particularly iron and magnesium. Chocolate gives instant boost of energy because of its sugar content, hence, should be drunk in moderation.

13. Strawberry Atole

Atole is pre-Hispanic. It is a very thick beverage consisting of masa harina and milk or water. Sweetened with sugar and flavoured with crushed fruit and spices, this healthy popular beverage is enjoyed throughout Mexico. There are many variants, different thickening agents and flavouring spices. Traditionally, it is consumed on cold mornings and is often accompanied with steamed corn dumplings/tamales.

You Require: **Cooking Time:** 15 minutes.

Strawberry crush	½ to ¾ cup	Sugar	¼ cup
Skimmed milk	2 cups	Water	2 cups
Corn flour	3 tbsp		

Preparation and Cooking:

1. Place strawberry crush, sugar and milk in a blender jar and blend until smooth. Remove into a cooking vessel.
2. Mix corn flour with 1 cup water, add remaining water. Place the mixture on fire and bring it to the boiling point, stirring constantly.

3. Pour over fruit mixture and simmer for 10 minutes on low fire, stirring all the way.

Serving: Serve immediately in individual mugs/cups.

Tips: Strawberries are an excellent source of pectin and soluble fibre that eliminate cholesterol. They are also rich in antioxidant nutrients, hence, an exceptional source of vitamin C. They are low in sodium and high in potassium.

14. Hot Punch

This is the most popular drink served in Mexico during X-mas and New Year festivities. It is prepared with seasonal fruits cooked in water with cinnamon and raw sugar. "Adults drink punch laced with alcohol", says Fresh Mexican.

You Require: **Cooking Time:** 45 minutes or so.

Water	11 cups	Prunes pitted	8 to 10 nos.
Apricots dried	10 to 12	Guavas	2 to 3 nos.
Hibiscus flowers dried	50 gm	Apple cored	1 no.
Raisins	1 tbsp	Cinnamon	2 sticks of 2" each
Sugarcane stalks	12' piece (opt)	Raw/castor sugar	½ cup or to taste
Rum	¾ cup or to taste		

Preparation and cooking:

1. Slice apple and guava into thick wedges (8 each).
2. Cut sugarcane stick into 2" long strips.
3. Boil 4 cups water, add hibiscus flowers and simmer for 15 minutes. Remove from fire and leave to infuse for 30 minutes or so.
4. Simultaneously, bring the remaining water to a boil in a large vessel over high heat and add prunes and apricots; lower the heat to medium and simmer for 10 minutes.
5. Add the apple, guavas, sugarcane strips, raisins, sugar and cinnamon stick, and simmer for 30 minutes on low heat. Stir in between for 2 to 3 times. Strain hibiscus water in the simmering mixture and discard the flowers.
6. Taste the punch, add more sugar, if required, and stir well.

Serving: Remove from heat and add rum to your liking. Ladle into individual mugs and serve hot immediately.

Main Course

Main course dishes are mostly the grilled or baked vegetables or a variety of meat steaks served with vegetables, seeds and nuts-based sauces either on the bed of simple, yellow, red or green rice or along with corn/wheat tortillas. Tortillas are used to make many dishes. A variety of breads too are included, and are used for assembling interesting and satisfying Cemita and Tortas etc.

1. Chicken Mexicana

(Pollo Mexican)

A simple chicken preparation, cooked often in Mexican households and enjoyed in day to day meals.

You Require: **Cooking Time:** 50 minutes.

Chicken	1 no.	Butter/cooking oil	¼ cup
Flour	1 tbsp	Salt	1 tsp
Tomato puree	2 cups	Tomatoes sliced	1 cup
Worcestershire sauce	2 tbsp	Onion sliced	1 no. medium
Crushed pepper	1 tsp	Chilli powder	1 tsp

Freshly cooked rice or tortillas to serve with.

Preparation and Cooking:

1. Wash and cut chicken into 8 pieces; dry with kitchen towel and keep aside.
2. Heat a non-stick heavy bottomed pan and add fat.
3. Add chicken pieces and brown nicely from all sides. Lift the pieces and keep them covered.
4. Blend flour with fat in the pan; add onions and tomatoes, cook for 1 minute; sprinkle salt, pepper and chilli powder; stir well; add tomato puree and chicken pieces; stir well and cover the dish.
5. Bring it to the boiling point and reduce the heat; simmer it for 40 to 45 minutes.
6. Stir gently twice in between; sprinkle ¼ cup water if chicken is not tender enough and cook for 10 minutes more.

Serving: Serve Chicken Mexicana hot with rice or corn/wheat tortillas as a main dish.

Tips: Instead of sliced onion, tomato and tomato puree, use 2 cups of red Tomato Salsa mixed with ½ cup water or canned tomato to cook chicken.

2. Toastada

Toastada is Spanish for 'toasted'; any fried or baked until crisp tortilla can be called toastada. In Mexico they are found in all sizes, from 1-inch to 12 inches; 1-inch ones are ideal to be used as bite sized canapés; 4 to 6 inch ones are regularly used for popular toastadas; and 12-inch ones are generally cut into triangles to be baked or fried as chips and then served with salsas, etc. The large ones are also topped with various cold and hot preparations like ceviches, guacamoles and meats stewed in different sauces. One of the most popular toastadas, easily recognized everywhere, is a crisp tortilla spread with a layer of refried beans, then topped with shredded lettuce and garnished with shredded vegetables or meats. The top is drizzled with sour cream, sprinkled with grated cheese and chopped cilantro and then topped with adobo or pickled jalapeno. Such toastadas are generally served in sets of three whether at home or in a traditional restaurant as a main meal. But as an appetizer, only one is served.

You Require: **Cooking Time:** 5 minutes for each toastada.

Tortillas	6 nos.	Vegetable oil	2 tbsp
Refried beans	3 cups	Cheese grated	1 and ½ cup
Chicken shredded	2 cups (opt)	Adobo/Enchilada sauce	1 cup
Finely chopped salad material	2 cups		

Preparation and Cooking:

1. Place a basic tortilla in a heavy non-stick pan that has been lightly oiled. Turn it over with a spatula till it is thoroughly warm. Remove and place it in a plate.
2. Put ½ inch to 1 inch thick layer of cooked and mashed kidney beans or baked beans on the tortilla.
3. Add finely chopped salad material or shredded chicken on top of it.
4. Sprinkle toastada with generous amount of grated cheese.
6. Finally, top it with Enchilada sauce or adobo and serve.

Serving: Serve it immediately as a snack or appetizer.

Place 2 more warm tortillas under this and serve it as a meal with soup and other accompaniments.

Tips: The salad material can include shredded lettuce/salad leaves/cabbage, spinach, carrot, finely chopped onions or spring onions, cucumber and tomato, sliced mushrooms, peppers and celery, etc.

3. Barbecued Chicken

Barbecued meats and vegetables are fondly enjoyed all over the country and this is one such dish that is easy to cook and excellent to eat.

You Require: **Cooking Time:** 1 hour 15 minutes.

Chicken	1 no.	Fat/salad oil	1/3 cup
Worcestershire sauce	¼ cup	Vinegar	2 tbsp
Sugar	2 tbsp	Tomato ketchup	½ cup
Tabasco	1 tsp	Garlic chopped fine	1 tbsp
Onion chopped	1 no. medium		
A piece of cheese cloth			

Preparation and Cooking:

1. Wash the whole chicken and dry with a kitchen towel or cut chicken in 4 pieces; dry with kitchen towel and keep aside.
2. Combine rest of the ingredients, except garlic and onion and marinate chicken with it. Stand it for 30 minutes to 1 hour.
3. Place the chicken in a heavy bottomed pan with a lid; tie garlic and onion in the cheese cloth like bouquet-garni and place in the pan and cover.
4. Cook the chicken on medium fire for 1 hour, turning 3 times at least.
5. Check if the chicken is done.
6. Remove cheese cloth before serving and squeeze it over the chicken.

Serving: Serve it hot as an appetizer or a part of the main dish with a good salad.

Tips: You may bake the marinated chicken in hot oven for 40 to 45 minutes or till done, turning once in between. Later, remove from the oven and wrap in foil to keep it warm. Use the leftover chicken later shredded in salads or in Mexican wraps, Burritos or Enchiladas.

4. La Casa Dia/Quesadilla

(Mushroom Keseidiayas)

Quesadilla is made by spreading one basic tortilla in a lightly oiled pan and stuffed lightly with any filling and generous helping of cheese on one half and the other half of the tortilla is then folded over and cooked. Each tortilla is cooked for 1 to 2 minutes, so that cheese inside melts and tortilla is warm enough.

You require: **Cooking Time:** 30 minutes.

Corn or flour tortillas	8 nos.	Mushroom sliced	250 gm
Red pepper sliced	½ no	Jalapeno sliced	2 nos.
Green pepper sliced	1 no.	Onions sliced	2 nos.
Garlic chopped	1 tbsp	Coriander chopped	¼ cup
Tomato sauce	2 tbsp	Low fat cheese slices	8 nos.

Mozerella/cheddar cheese grated	1 or ½ cup	Corn steamed	½ cup (opt)
Salt-n-pepper	to taste	Olive oil	2 to 3 tbsp

Red/green or both salsas to serve with.

Preparation and Cooking:

1. Heat olive oil in a pan and sauté onion and garlic in it; mix mushroom and cook for 1 minute; add red and green peppers and cook for a few seconds; sprinkle salt and pepper; add corn, mix well and cook till dry. Mix tomato sauce with it and sprinkle coriander. Cool the mixture and divide it into 8 parts.
2. Oil a heavy non-stick pan lightly with oil and heat it.
3. Place one cheese slice on one side of a basic tortilla or sprinkle grated cheese generously; spread one part mushroom filling and fold it into half. Do not overload quesadillas with stuffing.

Note: Amul brand of cheese in India is quite ideal for the preparations.

Place folded tortilla on the heated pan and cook it from both the sides; keep turning it on low fire with a spatula until cheese inside is slightly melted and tortilla is warm enough. Pick it up and serve.

Serving: Serve La Casa Dia warm with any salsa or tomato sauce. It can be eaten up like a sandwich. Any soup accompanies well with it.

Variation: Non-vegetarians can add fully cooked shredded chicken or cooked mince along with or without mushrooms and go ahead.

Tips: The quesadillas are very much a part of Mexican life. It is eaten as a meal or as a snack. It is sold on the roads for the benefit of working people. At home, quesadillas and soup make a dinner; and a ham and cheese, mushrooms and vegetables plus cheese can be a breakfast. They (small-sized quesadillas) make excellent appetizers. They are ideal for the parties too, as they can be prepared and assembled much in advance, overlapped in a baking tray, covered with paper towels and then with plastic wrap and refrigerated. Take them out 1 hour before use, warm them up as explained in the recipe, and serve.

The name 'Quesadilla' comes from the word 'Queso', which means 'cheese'; traditionally, the cheese used was a relatively mild cheese that melts well, but now in Mexico also 'mozzarella' (commonly, it is known as pizza cheese) too is used.

5 . Mexican Wraps

(Fajitas/Fahitaas)

Wraps or Fajitas are prepared with maize flour or wheat tortillas. Tortillas are filled or stuffed with vegetarian or non-vegetarian filling; wrapped and served with red and green salsas or Tabasco as a meal. Mostly, various fillings are placed on the table with tortillas and everyone makes his or her own wrap or a roll.

Main Course

Adobo Chicken in Pumpkin Seed Sauce, 104

Baked Eggs-n-Spinach, 130

Mexican Wraps, 96

Chicken Mexicana, 93

Deviled Chicken, 102

Enchiladas, 98

Mexican Green Rice, 112

Budin, 125

Mixiote de Pollo, 109

Peanut Crusted Fish with Pineapple Sauce, 120

Toastada, 94

Prawns in Red Sauce, 107

Rancheros, 100

Picnic Casserole, 114

Quesadilla, 95

Corn and Rice Casserole, 99

Sautéd Chicken, 100

Corn Savoury Cake, 103

Spicy Chicken Legs, 101

Barbecued Chicken, 94

Meatballs in Chilli Sauce, 106

Chimichangas, 108

Arozo Adobado, 113

Burritos, 117

Two Crust Beans Pie, 115

Garlic-flavoured Lemon Beans, 116

Yellow Rice, 114

Chicken with Pistachio Nuts Sauce, 118

Green, Red and Yellow Peppers Stuffed, 122

Mexican Style Pasta, 121

Courgette Mexican, 124

Roasted Eggplant, 124

Green Beans Omelette, 126

Stuffed Chillies in Ranchera Sauce, 129

Chocolate Chicken, 128

Fish in Pine Nut Sauce

Adobo Chicken with Pumpkin Seeds Sauce, 104

You Require: **Cooking Time:** In this recipe, cooking time cannot be specified

Large flour or wheat tortillas	8 no.	Boiled or broiled chicken cubes	2 cups
Cooked and mashed kidney beans	1 cup	Grated cheese	1 cup
Cooked rice	1 and ½ cup	Onion chopped fine	1 cup
Tomato deseeded and chopped	1 cup	Lettuce shredded	1 cup
Boiled corn kernels	1 cup	Red tomato salsa	1 cup
Green tomato salsa	1 cup	Red /green pepper chopped fine	1 cup
Sour cream	1 cup	Hot pepper sauce	¼ cup (opt)

Assembly and serving:

1. Keep the cooked ingredients warm.
2. Heat flour tortilla; spread sour cream on it and stuff with all or any combination of the above-mentioned ingredients and wrap. Prepare the rest of the wraps the same way. Wrap them like pockets or rolls and serve.

Serving: Serve additional salsa and sauces along.

Variation: Sauté onion and garlic in butter or olive oil; add boneless shredded and seasoned chicken or mushrooms and stir for 2 to 3 minutes. Sprinkle wine vinegar, chopped coriander or parsley and flavour it with adobo sauce. Mix properly and keep it warm as a filling.

Tips: The term 'Fajitas' is pronounced 'Fahitas' as here **j** is pronounced as **h**.

Cooking time: In this recipe, cooking time cannot be specified.

6. Charred Chillies Stuffed

(Chilli Rellenos)

You Require: **Cooking Time:** 1 hour.

Poblano chillies	6 nos.	Vinegar	2 tbsp
Or Indian achari mirch		Salt	1 tsp
Potato boiled	1 no.	Carrot grated	1 no.
Onion chopped	1 no small	Or Pepper chopped fine	½ no.
Rice cooked	½ cup (opt)	Cheese grated	2 tbsp
Chilli chopped fine	1 no.	Parsley chopped	2 tbsp
Vinegar	1 tsp	Pepper powder	1 tsp (opt)
Olive oil	1 tbsp	Salt	to taste

Ranchera sauce: 1 recipe to serve with

Preparation and Cooking:

1. Wash and dry the chillies; slit open and remove the seeds without damaging the shells.
2. Mix 2 tbsp vinegar and a little salt and with a brush, apply the mixture inside and outside the chillies. Stand for 30 minutes.
3. Meantime mash potato; heat oil and sauté onion and green chilli; add grated carrot, rice, cheese, parsley, vinegar, salt and pepper. Mix well and check the seasonings.
4. Divide the mixture into equal parts and stuff chillies one by one.
5. Now roast chillies directly over naked flame of the gas, one at a time till the black marks appear on top. Use a pair of tongs for holding chillies on the flame.
6. Arrange the stuffed chillies in a shallow serving plate.
7. Heat 1-tbsp oil in a pan; add ranchera sauce and heat up. Pour it around the stuffed chillies and garnish with chopped parsley.

Serving: Serve with any Mexican meal as a side dish.

Variation: Make a batter with ¼ cup corn flour and water of thick pouring consistency and season it. Stand it for 10 minutes. Meantime, heat oil for frying; dip each stuffed chilli in the batter and shallow fry on medium heat, turning the sides till golden in colour. Drain on kitchen paper and serve hot with any main meal.

You may mix cooked minced meat with mashed potato and fill the chillies with it.

7. Enchiladas

Enchiladas are tortillas which are dipped in enchilada sauce, stuffed and rolled cylindrically (to make a tube), topped with cheese and baked to be served as a main meal.

You Require: **Cooking Time for Enchilada sauce:** 15 minutes.

For Enchilada sauce:

Tomato sauce	1 cup	Water	2 to 2 and ½ cups
Chilli powder	3 tbsp	Corn oil/cooking oil	3 tbsp
Corn meal	2 tbsp leveled		

For stuffing:

Grated cheese	2 cups	Spring onions with greens	2 cups

Refried beans or tinned-baked beans mixed with cheese, onion and herbs

Cooking for Enchilada sauce:

1. Heat oil for sauce and brown cornmeal slightly in it.
2. Add rest of the ingredients and cook for 10 minutes on medium fire, stirring constantly to avoid lumps.
3. Keep it warm.
4. Preheat the oven for moderate heat.

Assembly:

1. Dip each tortilla in hot enchilada sauce and keep it in the plate. Continue until all the tortillas are dipped.
2. Remove each tortilla one by one, spread on the chopped onions and grated cheese and beans mixture.
3. Roll the tortilla and place in a baking dish.
4. Pour the remaining sauce over the enchiladas in the baking dish and sprinkle some more cheese over it.
5. Heat in the hot oven till cheese is melted.

Serving: Serve the hot enchiladas with tossed green salad and baked beans as a meal.

Information: "Enchilada, literally, means 'chilled tortilla'. In other words, a tortilla rubbed, mixed, cooked with, soaked in or otherwise flavoured with chillies of one type or another", says Roberto Santibanez. He further says that there are many variations. "The masa (dough) for the tortillas can be made with chilli paste or broth and then made into tortillas, or uncooked red masa tortillas are filled with cheese, then fried and served with an assortment of salsas and toppings, which can include scrambled eggs. Nowadays in Mexico, the modern concept of enchilada means corn masa tortillas, topped or filled with seafood, poultry, meat/vegetables and served with any variety of chilli-based sauces or salsas. They are usually garnished with greens, herbs, vegetables, grated cheesem etc.".

8. Corn and Rice Casserole

You Require: **Cooking Time:** 40 to 45 minutes.

Long grain rice	1 and ½ cup	Water	3 cups
Salt	2 tsp leveled	Cream style corn	1 can
Hard boiled eggs or potatoes	4 nos. (opt)	Butter	2 tbsp
Parsley or coriander chopped	3 tbsp	Pepper	to taste
Kashmiri chilli powder	2 tsp		

Preparation and Cooking:

1. Wash and drain rice.
2. Cut eggs into halves and keep aside.
3. Boil 3 cups of water in a pan; add salt and rice; bring it to the boiling point; reduce the heat and cover the pan. Cook rice on low heat till rice is tender but not mushy (for almost 30 minutes).
4. Preheat an oven for moderate heat.

5. Place corn in a pan; add 1 tbsp butter and seasonings and heat it thoroughly.
6. Transfer the cooked rice in a baking dish and make a well in the center. Gently spoon the corn in the center and arrange the eggs on the corn.
7. Sprinkle parsley over the eggs.
8. Sprinkle chilli powder over the rice.
9. Heat butter and drizzle on top.
10. Bake in a preheated oven till corn is bubbly and the dish is heated through.
11. Or cover the dish with cling film and heat on the REHEAT mode of a microwave for 4 to 5 minutes.

Serving: Serve the dish hot with any sauce.

9. Sautéd Chicken

An easy recipe to cook chicken and vegetables and enjoy the goodness of both sautéd meat and vegetables together for the maintenance of health.

You Require: **Cooking Time:** 40 minutes.

Chicken legs	8 nos.	Capsicums	3 large
Tomatoes	3 large	Garlic	4 to 6 cloves
Mushrooms	200 gm	Butter	4 tbsp
Salt	to taste	White vinegar/white wine	¼ cup
Adobo	2 tsp	Olive oil	1 tbsp

Preparation and Cooking:

1. Wash chicken legs and dry with kitchen towel; prick them with fork all over and marinate with wine or vinegar, salt, pepper, adobo and oil for 30 minutes to 1 hour.
2. Crush garlic and chop mushrooms, capsicums and tomatoes.
3. Heat 3 tbsp butter; add crushed garlic; fry and discard. Add chicken and cook till almost done. Save the marinade liquid.
4. In another pan, heat 1 tbsp butter and sauté chopped vegetables; sprinkle a little salt and pepper and mix lightly.
5. Mix chicken with hot sautéd vegetables and add saved marinade liquid. Mix it well.

Serving: Serve it hot with Corn Fritters and Cilantro soup.

10. Rancheros

This is a classic dish of the Mexican breakfast menu. In this internationally famous dish, single fried eggs are placed on a warmed corn tortilla and then covered with delicious tomato sauce. "Traditionally, it is also served with black beans and extra tortilla or crusty white bread to mop up every bit of the delicious sauce".

You Require: **Cooking Time:** Almost 20 minutes to cook Ranchera sauce.

Soft corn tortillas	8 nos.	Cooking oil	2 tbsp
Eggs	8 nos.	Ranchera sauce	2 cups

Preparation and Cooking:

1. Preheat a heavy-based non-stick pan over a medium heat; brush the tortillas with oil and warm each side of 2 to 3 tortillas at a time almost for 30 seconds (each side). Cover them with a foil or cotton kitchen napkin (folded) and place in a large casserole to keep them warm.
2. Brush a small non-stick pan with a little oil and heat it up over a medium heat; break 2 eggs at a time in it and cook over a low heat till the whites of the eggs are set.

Serving: Place two tortillas in each plate and place 2 cooked eggs on top; spoon Ranchera sauce generously over the whites of the eggs, sprinkle a little parsley over that and serve it immediately.

You may serve another tortilla along with it. Generally, in Mexico, they serve 3 tortillas together for this dish, in particular.

Tips: Tortillas can be prepared the previous day and stored under refrigeration and the sauce can be cooked fresh to serve this dish at breakfast. Even the sauce can be cooked and stored beforehand. Warm it covered, in a microwave, and season it before use.

Many people deep fry the tortillas for the dish but warming them up after brushing with oil is lighter on heart.

11. Spicy Chicken Legs

Since poultry is enjoyed all over the country in variety of ways, here is another very easy-to-cook recipe to prepare a spicy and flavourful dish with the most common ingredients.

You Require: **Cooking Time:** 45 minutes.

Chicken legs	8 nos. large	Egg	2 nos.
Flour	½ cup	Curry powder	2 tsp
Cinnamon powder	1 tsp	Mustard powder	2 tsp
Pepper powder	2 tsp	Vinegar	2 tbsp
Salt	to taste	Oil for frying	

Kashmiri red chilli powder or any other red chilli powder of your preference: 2 tsp

Preparation and Cooking:

1. Clean chicken legs, prick them with a fork all over; apply salt, vinegar and 1 tsp pepper and keep it aside for 2 hours.

2. Beat eggs and keep aside.
3. Combine all the dry ingredients of the recipe together.
4. Coat chicken legs first with beaten eggs and then roll in dry ingredients.
5. Preheat the oven.
6. Heat oil and fry legs on medium fire till golden brown and well cooked. Drain on kitchen oil absorbent paper. Avoid frying chicken in very hot oil, otherwise, it will be browned fast and remains uncooked from inside.
7. Place chicken legs in a baking tray; cover with foil and bake in the hot oven for 5 minutes; uncover and bake for another 5 minutes.

Serving: Serve 'Spicy Chicken Legs', hot with Mexican vegetable salad.

12. Deviled Chicken

Another delicacy of chicken to be relished with rice preparation any time throughout the year.

You Require: **Cooking Time:** 1 hour and 15 minutes.

Chicken	1000 gm	Salt-n-pepper	to taste
Oil/butter to brush the chicken			

For Deviled sauce:

Onions minced	4 nos.	Garlic crushed	4 cloves
Bouquet garni	1 small bag	Chicken stock	3 cups
White pepper	½ tsp	Butter	3 tbsp
Flour	3 tbsp	Curry powder	1 tsp
Water	1 tbsp	Worcestershire sauce	1 tbsp
Tomato puree	1 tbsp	Tabasco green	1 tbsp

Basic white rice 1 recipe to serve with

Preparation and Cooking:

1. Preheat oven for 200 degrees Celsius.
2. Line a shallow roasting pan with aluminium foil.
3. Combine oil, salt and pepper and brush the chicken (with skin) inside and outside with it lightly.
4. Place it in the prepared pan and cover it loosely with foil; and bake it for 1 hour or till tender. Do not seal chicken with foil.
5. Remove the pan from the oven and let the chicken be cooled enough to be handled easily.
6. Remove and discard the skin. Cut the chicken into 8 pieces and arrange on ovenproof platter. If you like you may remove the chicken from the bones and place on a platter.
7. Cover the platter with foil and keep the chicken warm.

Cooking for Deviled sauce:

1. Combine onion, garlic, bouquet garni, pepper and 2 cups of stock in a pan and simmer for 20 minutes and pass the onion mixture through a sieve. Add enough stock to make the liquid 2 cups.
2. Melt butter in another pan; blend in flour and stir; add onion mixture gradually, stirring all the time. Combine curry powder and 1 tbsp water to make a smooth paste.
3. Now add curry paste, Worcestershire sauce, Tabasco and tomato puree to the cooking sauce. Cook stirring frequently until thick and smooth.

Serving: line a serving platter with cooked rice; dot the rice with butter; arrange the cooked chicken pieces over it and pour over the hot Deviled sauce. Serve immediately with Beans salad.

Tips: You may cook Deviled sauce in advance or when chicken is being baked initially.

13. Corn Savoury Cake

Corn cake, sweet or savoury, is baked all over Mexico throughout the year but especially in harvest season it is enjoyed more. It is a good source of protein and rich in fibre. It is usually served for breakfast or dinner with coffee or hot chocolate.

You Require: **Cooking Time:** 45 to 50 minutes.

Fresh corn kernels	500 gm	Onion chopped	1 nos.
Green chilli roasted	2 to 3 nos.	Black Olives	5 nos.
Garlic roasted	10 to 12 flakes	Butter	¼ cup
Capsicum chopped	1 no.	Eggs	3 nos.
Baking powder	1 tsp	Salt	2 tsp
Peppercorns crushed	1 tsp	Mint (fresh)	¼ cup

Preparation and Cooking:

1. Slice olives and keep aside.
2. Preheat an oven for moderate heat.
3. Grease a loaf tin or a rectangular/square glass dish.
4. Place corn kernels and eggs in the blender and blend well until smooth.
5. Melt butter slightly and add to the corn mixture.
6. Add rest of the ingredients and blend for a few seconds.
7. Pour the corn mixture in the greased tin or in a dish and decorate with sliced olives.
8. Bake in the centre of a hot oven for 40 to 45 minutes or till done. Insert a needle in the centre of the cake, if it comes out clean, switch off the heat and leave the dish inside the oven for 5 minutes.

9. Remove the dish and cool. Run a tip of a palate knife around the edge of the tin to loosen the cake and invert it on to a plate. Invert it once more, so that the garnished side is up.

Serving: Slice it and serve as a savoury with coffee or as a side dish with chilli strips or sauces.

Variation: Make sweet corn cake. Use 500 gm corn, 60 gm butter, 70 gm castor sugar, 70 gm flour, 3 eggs, 1 tsp baking powder and ¼ tsp salt to make sweet cake and sprinkle the finished cake with 2 tbsp icing sugar.

14. Adobo marinated Chicken with Pumpkin/Melon Seed Sauce

Gourmets' delight, this dish is a speciality mostly cooked on feasts and festivals.

You Require: **Cooking Time:** 45 minutes.

Chicken cut in 4 pieces	1 no.	Adobo sauce	¼ cup
Lemon juice	from 1 lemon	Oregano	1 tsp
Olive oil	1 tbsp	Salt	1 tsp
For the sauce:			
Melon seeds or Pumpkin seeds	½ cup	Onion chopped	1 no.
Garlic chopped	2 tbsp	Green chillies	2 no.
Olive oil	2 tbsp		
Tomatoes chopped (roasted and skinned)	2 large		
Roasted cumin powder	1 tsp	Clove powder	1 tsp
Pepper powder	1 tsp	Bay leaf	1 no.
Salt	to taste	Parsley chopped	2 tbsp
Chicken stock/water	2 cups		

Preparation and Cooking:

1. Clean chicken and make gashes with a sharp knife. Combine abodo sauce, lemon juice, oil and seasonings together and rub it nicely on chicken pieces; cover and stand it for 6 to 8 hours or refrigerate overnight. Take out the chicken 30 minutes in advance if refrigerated.
2. Preheat an oven and take out the chicken 30 minutes in advance if refrigerated.
3. Pick up the chicken pieces from the marinade (saving it for later use) and place them in a baking tray; cover the tray with aluminium foil and bake it in a moderately hot oven for 30 to 35 minutes or till done. Check it once and turn the side of chicken pieces. Once cooked, drain the liquid, if any, in a bowl and keep the chicken covered and warm.
4. When the chicken is being cooked, make the sauce.
5. **Roast the seeds:** Place pumpkin seeds or melon seeds in a small paper bag and place in the microwave, cook on micro medium (80% power) for 2 to 2 and ½ minutes or till crackled, shaking the bag once in between. Cool and powder, saving 1 tsp for garnishing. You may roast the seeds in a pan or on griddle till they start crackling.

6. Heat oil in a heavy-based pan; sauté onion in it; add garlic and green chilli, cook for a few seconds and add tomatoes and further cook for 2 minutes; switch off the heat.
7. Cool the mixture slightly; mix the marinating mixture with it and pass through a liquidizer; add half the stock, If needed; strain the puree through a sieve if the mixture is not very smooth.
8. Mix the seed powder with the puree and return it to fire; add rest of the stock, bay leaf, cumin and clove powders and salt. Bring it to the boiling point and lower the heat. Simmer gravy for 10 to 15 minutes or till the sauce is nice and shining. Add chopped parsley and keep the sauce covered.

Serving: Put gravy in a heated serving dish; place cooked chicken over it and garnish the dish with saved roasted seeds. Serve it hot with white/green Mexican rice or any kind of bread. It is delicious with both.

Variations: *Serve the **marinated and baked Fish or sautéd Prawns** with this gravy.

*Even grilled **Paneer chunks** can be added to it. Add sautéd prawns or paneer pieces in the gravy; cover the dish and reheat for 2 minutes in a microwave. Or heat in a pan with additional 1/4 cup water for 5 minutes.

Vegetarian delicacy: Remove the bitter juices of **Egg plant roundels**; deep fry them and arrange in a dish; pour melon or pumpkin seeds sauce over them; sprinkle grated cheese and bake in a hot oven till cheese is melted.

15. Pescado en Pesto Verde

(Fish in Pine Nut Sauce)

Pine nut sauce is prepared on special occasions. This delicate sauce, made with ground pine nuts with a little chilli incorporated in it, lends very aromatic flavour to the dish and its greenish creamy colour, a nice appearance to the preparation. Pine nuts are a good source of dietary fiber, essential for good health.

You Require: **Cooking Time:** 45 minutes.

Fish fillets	4 nos. 100 gm each	Lemon juice	3 tbsp
Vegetable oil	1 tbsp	Freshly ground pepper	1 tsp
Salt	to taste		

For Pine nuts sauce:

Pine nuts	130 gm + 20 gm	Onion chopped	1 no.
Green chillies	3 nos. (deseeded and chopped)	Garlic chopped	2 cloves
Basil leaves	¼ cup	White pepper	1 tsp
Salt	to taste	Cooking oil	2 tbsp
Veg. stock/water	1 cup	Lemon juice	1 tbsp (opt)

Preparation and Cooking:

1. Mix together lemon juice, vegetable oil, salt and pepper to marinade fish with it. Apply the marinade on the fish nicely, cover and keep it aside for 1 hour under refrigeration.
2. Toast 20 gm pine nuts lightly and keep aside.
3. Either bake the fish in hot oven for 30 to 40 minutes, changing the side once after 20 minutes or grill it till done. Switch off the oven. Keep it covered with a piece of foil in the oven to keep it warm.
4. When fish is being marinated and getting cooked, make pesto sauce.
5. Heat oil in a heavy-bottomed pan; sauté onion in it, add garlic and green chillies and cook for 1 minute. Transfer the onion mixture to the blender; add stock and pine nuts; throw in basil and blend until smooth.
6. Cook the sauce on medium flame for 10 minutes or so; add a little more water if the sauce appears too thick. Season it with salt, pepper and lemon juice.
7. Check the seasonings and if need be, add a few drops of green Tabasco.
8. Pour the sauce over the cooked fish kept warm in the oven.

Serving: Arrange the fish over the Red Mexican rice in a platter; place half the fish on top of the rice; pour some sauce over it and top with rest of the fish. Garnish it with basil and toasted pine nuts. Serve it hot.

You may serve it in individual plates.

Variations:

1. Serve roasted chicken breast with Pesto sauce.
2. Serve the fish with Yellow or White rice.
3. Serve fried or shallow fried slices of Zucchini with Pesto sauce and garnish with cottage cheese and pine nuts.

16. Meatballs in Chilli Sauce

This delicious dish is not only easier to cook but also contains very high nutritional value and is very popular in homes as well as in restaurants.

You Require: **Cooking Time:** 40 minutes to 1 hour.

Minced mutton (without fat)	500 gm	Onion chopped fine	1 no. small
Garlic crushed	1 clove	Coriander chopped fine	¼ cup
Egg	1 no.	Salt	to taste
Freshly crushed pepper	2 tsp leveled		

For Chilli sauce:

Red chillies dry	4 nos.	Onion chopped	1 no. small

Or Chipotle chillies	3 nos.	Tomatoes	5 to 6 nos.
Garlic peeled	1 clove	Bay leaf	1 no.
Thyme	1 sprig	Salt	to taste
Mutton stock/water	2 cups	Parsley chopped	2 tbsp

Preparation and Cooking:

1. Deseed the chillies; roast them in a heavy based pan for a few seconds from both sides over medium fire and soak them in 1 cup warm water for 20 minutes.
2. Meantime, on hot griddle, dry fry chopped onion and garlic till soft.
3. Roast tomatoes on naked flame one by one; remove the skin and roughly chop them.
4. Drain chillies (saving the soaking water) and place them in a blender; add tomatoes, onion and garlic too; add the soaking liquid and blend to a smooth puree. Pass through a sieve if the puree is not very smooth.
5. Heat the oil in a heavy based pan; add tomato chilli puree and stock or water; cook it on medium fire along with bay leaf and thyme sprig for 15 to 20 minutes. Season to taste with salt and keep the sauce on slow fire.
6. **Now make the meat balls.** In a working bowl, combine minced meat, onion, garlic, egg, coriander, salt and pepper. Mix the mixture thoroughly with your hands; divide the mixture into equal sized balls and shape them into small balls.
7. Drop the balls into the hot sauce and bring it to the boiling point; cover it and cook for 30 to 35 minutes or till balls are tender.
8. Or gently transfer the sauce with meat balls into a micro safe bowl; cover it with a lid and cook in a microwave on HIGH for 8 to 10 minutes. Stand it for 5 minutes and then serve.

Serving: Garnish the meat balls with parsley and serve with plain rice or Green rice.

Even the warm Tortillas are one of the best accompaniments.

Tips: You can use lean pork or beef mince instead of mutton mince and follow the recipe as it is.

17. Prawns in Red Sauce

A spicy shellfish dish, accompanies excellently with plain white, green or yellow rice, and makes a balanced meal. Prawns are a good source of protein, essential minerals and vitamins required by the human body.

You Require: **Cooking Time:** 35 to 40 minutes.

Jumbo Prawns	12 nos.	Lemon juice	2 tbsp
Salt	½ tsp	Or White vinegar	2 tbsp

For Red sauce:

Red pepper	1 no.	Tomatoes roasted and chopped	4 nos.
Or Red chillies fresh	3 nos.	Onion chopped	1 no small
Garlic peeled	1 clove	Bay leaf	1 no.
Adobo sauce	¼ cup	Oregano dry	1 tsp
Veg stock or water	1 and ½ cup	Olive oil	2 tbsp
White pepper powder	1 tsp	Salt	to taste

Parsley or coriander for garnishing.

Plain white rice to serve with.

Preparation and Cooking:

1. Clean and de-vein prawns; marinade with lemon juice/vinegar and salt and keep aside for 30 minutes to 1 hour. Strain and discard the liquid.
2. Meantime slit and deseed chillies. Chop them roughly.
3. Heat oil in a pan and cook chopped onions and garlic till translucent; add chopped chillies and tomatoes; cook for 1 minute and switch off the fire.
4. Transfer the cooked mixture to a blender; add ½ cup stock and blend well.
5. Add adobo sauce and rest of the stock; blend once again and remove.
6. Transfer the blended mixture to a pan; add bay leaf, oregano, salt and pepper and let it cook on slow fire.
7. When the sauce is cooking, either place prawns on skewers, brush them with oil and cook under a grill for 6 minutes, changing the side by rotating the skewers and brushing the prawns; remove from skewers and place them in the sauce and cook further for 10 to 15 minutes; or sauté prawns in a non-stick pan with 1 tbsp oil in it and then place them in the cooking sauce. Cook for 10 to 15 minutes.
8. Remove from fire; check the seasonings; cover and stand it for 5 minutes.

Serving: Garnish prawns with chopped coriander or parsley and serve with or on plain White rice as the main dish.

Variation: Cut fish into small pieces; marinade; sauté in a non-stick pan gently and cook in the gravy.

18. Chimichangas

Chimichangas are the tortillas that are filled with any veg. or non-veg. filling and then folded like envelops and deep fried till crisp.

You Require: **Cooking Time:** 40 minutes.

Fresh flour tortillas	6 to 8 nos.	Mushrooms chopped	½ cup
Green pepper chopped	½ cup	Steamed corn kernels	1 cup
Cauliflower grated	½ cup	Or green peas	1 cup

Cooked meat of your choice	1 cup (opt)		
(shredded chicken, cooked-n-chopped shrimps, fish flakes or mutton mince, etc.)			
Spring onions with greens (chopped)	3 nos.	Green chillies chopped	2 to 3 nos.
Garlic chopped	1 tbsp	Tomato puree	2 tbsp
Parsley chopped	¼ cup	Oregano	1 tsp
Pepper	1 tsp	Adobo sauce	1 tbsp
Cheddar cheese grated	1 cup	Salt	to taste
Toothpicks	6 to 8 nos.	Oil for deep frying	

Preparation and Cooking:

1. Heat 2 tbsp oil in a large pan and sauté onion, garlic and chillies; add cauliflower and stir; add corn kernels or green peas; sprinkle a few drops of water and cover; cook for 5 minutes on medium fire; open the lid, add cooked meat of your choice (if using) and add tomato puree, oregano, salt and pepper. Stir gently. Remove from fire and add grated cheese and chopped parsley.
2. To cool the mixture, transfer it in a large plate.
3. Heat oil to a smoking point and then lower the heat.
4. Spread one flour tortilla on the working surface and place 2 to 3 tbsp filling and fold tortilla like an envelope.
5. Stick 1 tooth pick in the centre and fry it in hot oil till crisp. Drain on kitchen oil absorbent paper and serve hot. Thus, stuff and roll the remaining tortillas and fry till golden crisp. Remove the tooth pick before serving.

Serving: Serve the hot envelopes with any of the salsas and a soup as a main meal.

19. Mixiote de Pollo

(Chicken baked in Almond Sauce in Greased Paper)

The term 'Mixiote' means the tough outer papery skin of the leaves of maguey plant which is also called the century plant. In cooking they serve as a waterproof container for various ingredients. Traditionally, these leaves were to wrap the pieces of marinated meat with sauce into small parcels, tied with string. But nowadays, greaseproof paper/parchment paper is used instead.

You Require: **Cooking Time:** 1 hour 15 minutes.

Whole chicken legs	4 nos.	Adobo sauce	½ cup
Salt	½ tsp		

For Almond sauce:

Onion peeled and halved	1 no.	Tomatoes	2 nos.
Garlic unpeeled	2 cloves	Chilli sauce	2 tbsp

Cooking oil	1 tbsp	Almond	¼ cup
Oregano dried	½ tsp	Thyme dried	½ tsp
Salt	to taste	Chicken stock	1 and ½ cup

Squares of grease-proof paper pieces 4 of 15x15-inch pieces

Squares of grease-proof paper 4 pieces of 7x7-inch pieces

Four pieces of chicken twine 8 to 10 inches each in length

Preparation and Cooking:

1. Wash chicken legs; dry them with kitchen towel; with a sharp knife put a few gashes on the legs.
2. Mix together adobo sauce and salt and rub it nicely on chicken legs. Cover and keep overnight under refrigeration. Take it out from the refrigerator 2 hours before use.
3. Powder almonds and keep aside.
4. Heat a non-stick pan or a griddle and roast onion, garlic and tomatoes till soft, turning many times in between. Cool and peel the garlic. Roughly chop onion and tomatoes. Place the roasted ingredients in a blender; add ½ cup stock and blend well. Add powdered almonds and rest of the stock; blend once more and pass through a not so fine sieve.
5. Heat the oil in a heavy bottomed pan; add the pureed mixture, chilli sauce and herbs and simmer for 15 to 20 minutes. Add salt and mix well. Cool.
6. Preheat an oven for moderate heat.

Assembling the bundles:

1. Spread one square of 15 inches on the working platform; place one 7-inch paper in the centre of that; keep 1-leg piece in the centre and pour a little almond sauce on top of the chicken; turn the leg and put some sauce on it too. Gather the sides and tie the packet securely with the twine. Finish assembling all the bundles in the same fashion.
2. Place the bundles in an oven-proof dish inside a large roasting tin half filled with hot water. Make sure that water does not touch the parcels.

   You may place a cooling rack in the large roasting tin with water and place bundles of chicken.
3. Steam-bake the chicken bundles for 50 to 60 minutes or until the chicken is tender.

Serving: Serve hot. Transfer each packet to a shallow dish or a soup plate. Let each diner snip/open the string to untie the packet and enjoy fragrance of the dish. Warm Tortillas and Green Salsa are the best accompaniments.

Variation: Use boneless chicken and marinate it first with the almond sauce for a couple of hours (after 5th step) and then assemble in bundles.

In this case, cooking time will be reduced.

20. Simple White Rice

(Basic Recipe of White Rice)

Although corn and beans are considered indigenous in Mexico, rice is not. "It was introduced in the late 1500s by Spanish merchants, who were already familiar with rice. A tropical grain, rice thrived in Mexico's steamy central and southern provinces."

You Require: **Cooking Time:** 25 to 30 minutes.

Long-grain Basmati rice	2 cups	Water	4 cups
Whit onion chopped	1 small	Garlic clove	1 small
Vegetable oil	2 tbsp	Salt	1 to 2 tsp
Serrano chillies	2 nos.		
Or any other mild green chilli			

Preparation and Cooking:

1. Rinse the rice in a strainer and do not soak. Drain thoroughly. The grains of the rice should feel dry when touched.
2. Combine the garlic, onion and water with salt in a blender and blend well till smooth.
3. Heat oil in a heavy-based pan; lower the heat; add rice and stir-fry; increase the heat and cook till translucent.
4. Add blended and seasoned onion water and chillies; bring it to the boiling point and lower the heat. Cover the pan with a tight lid and cook until the rice is tender and all the liquid is absorbed. The whole process of cooking rice will take about 20 to 25 minutes.
5. Switch off the heat and let the rice stand for 10 minutes.
6. Remove the chillies; stir the rice with a fork before serving.

Serving: Serve the rice hot, immediately with any vegetarian or non-vegetarian dish as a main meal.

Tips: Mexicans never simply boil rice and serve. They fry it first in a little oil until slightly crisp to give texture and toasty flavour; and then they cook in seasoned water/vegetable or chicken stock or fish broth. They usually pick one of the two methods:

a) chopping the onion and garlic finely and sautéing them before adding the rice.
b) leaving the garlic cloves whole and onions in large pieces, so that they can be easily removed before serving the rice.

Note: Some of the good cooks even blend garlic and onion to add flavour and to make the preparation easier and save the trouble of picking the onion and garlic out of the finished dish.

21. Mexican Green Rice

(Arroz Verde)

Mexicans love colouring their rice in different colours by flavouring and seasoning them with different ingredients like vegetables, chillies and herbs, etc. Rice cooked in simple way following basic recipe and then seasoned after separating the grains, becomes special in an inexpensive way. Such a dish can be a part of the multicourse meals.

You Require: **Cooking Time:** 35 minutes.

Basmati rice	1 and ½ cup	Poblano chilli	1 no.
Capsicum	1 no.	Or green Achari mirch	2 nos.
Onion chopped roughly	1 no.	Coriander chopped	½ cup
Spinach puree	¼ cup	Olive oil	3 tbsp
Garlic	1 clove	Or butter	4 tbsp
French/butter beans chopped	½ to 1 cup	Salt	to taste
Water or chicken stock	3 cups if required		

Preparation and Cooking:

1. Wash and drain rice. Par-boil the rice in plenty of water with ½ tsp salt; drain and keep aside. Cool. Or take one recipe simple white rice (precooked and cooled) and follow rest of the recipe step by step.
2. Roast chillies and capsicum directly on naked flame; cool, clean, deseed and chop.
3. Roast garlic on hot griddle and peel.
4. Steam chopped beans in a microwave for 2 minutes on HIGH, remove and rinse with tap water. Keep aside.
5. Combine chopped chillies, capsicum, garlic, onion, coriander and spinach puree in a blender and grind with ¼ cup water.
6. Heat olive oil or butter in a big open pan or kadai; add the chilli coriander paste to it and cook till water dries up; add salt to taste and mix. Add rice and stir nicely but lightly, so that rice gets coated evenly with green paste and appear nicely green and shining.

Alternate: Do not parboil rice. After frying green paste, add washed rice to the paste and fry (as for Indian Pulaos) till the grains separate; add measured chicken stock or water; bring to the boiling point and lower the heat. Cook till the rice is soft. Fluff it with fork before serving.

Serving: Garnish the 'Arroz Verde' with beans and serve with veg or non-veg accompaniment.

Serve it with pickled vegetables.

Serve it with Chocolate chicken.

Variation: Cook green rice with stir fried Prawns or Shrimps in addition.

Tips: The rice can be boiled 1 day in advance and refrigerated; refrigerated and tossed with rest of the ingredients before serving. Presentation of pre-boiled rice, tossed later is very impressive, as each grain appears separate and colourful.

22. Arrozo Adobado

(Mexican Red Rice with Roasted Chicken)

The adobo sauce and red roasted pepper give the plain rice not only the beautiful brick colour but also great chilli flavour.

You Require: **Cooking Time:** 35 minutes.

Precooked Simple white rice	1 and ½ recipe	Or Pre-boiled rice	3 cups
Roasted chicken	1 no, cut into pieces	Or Shredded roasted chicken	3 cups
Seasoning ingredients:			
Adobo sauce	¼ cup	Onion chopped	1 no.
Tomatoes	2 nos.	Or Tomato puree	¼ cup
Red pepper roasted	½ no	Red pepper chopped	½ no
Olive/vegetable oil	¼ cup	Salt	to taste

Preparation and Cooking:

1. Roast, peel and chop tomatoes roughly.
2. Combine adobo sauce, tomatoes or tomato puree, onion and roasted red pepper in a grinder and grind to a paste. Add a little water, if needed, while grinding.
3. Heat oil in a big pan or kadai and fry red paste in it till the moisture evaporates; add salt and mix well; sprinkle rice over the red paste and stir gently, so that, the rice coats the red paste well. Add roasted chicken pieces/shredded chicken and chopped pepper. Stir for a while lightly or till the chicken is heated up.

Note: Previously prepared rice can be heated up in a microwave oven. Place rice in a micro safe dish, with a lid, sprinkle a few drops of water or chicken stock over the rice evenly, cover and heat through on micro High for 3 to 4 minutes.

Serving: Serve it hot with Chicken in Pista nut sauce.

Serve it with Fish in Pine nuts sauce.

Variation: Use stir fried prawns instead of shredded chicken.

Make vegetarian Red rice without chicken. Colour and flavour the simple white rice with the red paste made with seasoning ingredients; add strips of red pepper, mix gently and serve.

Tips: You may not use boiled rice, but add chicken stock to the red paste and cook rice in it as explained in Green rice. In this manner, add shredded chicken to the rice when rice is half done.

23. Yellow Rice

(Arroz Amarillo)

Creative chefs, inspired by global pantry, develop a lot of recipes which go very well with the authentic food of the country. This recipe is one such example of Mexican chefs.

You Require: **Cooking Time:** 10 minutes if the simple rice is precooked.

Simple white rice	1 recipe		

Flavouring and colouring ingredients:

Vegetable oil	2 tbsp	Scallions/leeks	3 medium
Serrano or green chilli	1 large	Garlic chopped	2 tbsp
Dijon mustard (prepared)	2 tbsp	Cilantro chopped	1/3 cup
Mint chopped	2 tbsp	Salt	½ tsp

Preparation and Cooking:

1. Trim and chop scallions or leek finely. Chop the chilli too.
2. Heat the oil in a pan over medium heat and add the onion, chilli and garlic, stir and cook till translucent.
3. Stir in the mustard and cook for 1 minute; stir in all the chopped ingredients and cook for 1 minute.
4. Toss rice with this mixture, add salt and mix thoroughly. Heat up rice slightly if cooked in advance.

Serving: Serve the rice hot at lunch/dinner.

24. Picnic Casserole

(Corn and Peppers Pie)

This inexpensive and easy-to-make corn pie is a vegetarians' delight. Served with a salad and a soup, this main dish makes an excellent meal.

You Require: **Cooking Time:** 1 and ½ hour for baking.

Cream style corn	1 cup	Roasted corn kernels	2 cups
Mixed chopped peppers (Green, red and yellow)	1 cup		
Olives black chopped fine	10 no.		
Garlic paste	1 tsp	Flour	½ cup
Corn meal	1 cup	Chilli powder	1 and ½ tsp
Salt	2 tsp	Pepper	½ tsp
Baking powder	½ tsp	Tomato sauce	½ cup

Milk	1 cup	Butter/Oil	½ cup
Eggs	3 nos.		

Preparation and Cooking:

1. Sift together flour, cornmeal, salt, chilli, pepper and baking powders.
2. Beat eggs.
3. Preheat the oven for moderate heat.
4. Combine cream style corn, roasted corn, tomato sauce, milk, fat and eggs together and stir.
5. Blend dry ingredients into corn mixture and mix well.
6. Add garlic, black olives (save 2 for garnishing) and mixed peppers.
7. Grease a large ovenproof dish and pour the mixture into it. Spread it properly. Garnish with olives and peppers.
8. Bake in moderately hot oven for 1 hour to 1 and ½ hours. Insert a needle in the centre and check the doneness. Needle should come out dry.

Serving: Serve this 'Corn and Peppers Pie' hot with any sauce as a main meal.

Tips: To get the roasted corn, roast 1 or 2 corn on the cobs (bhutta) directly on the naked flame of your gas stove; slightly cool and with a fruit knife remove the corn kernels from the cobs. Use in salad, soup or in any pie. You may use roasted corn even for filling as roasting enhances the taste of corn kernels.

25. Two Crust Beans and Mushroom Pie

Mexican pies are stuffed with a variety of fillings. Mostly, boiled kidney beans are combined with different vegetables like mushrooms, pumpkins and peppers and then flavoured with pickled vegetables, herbs and spices. Beans are also combined commonly with meats.

You Require: **Cooking Time:** 20 minutes for preparation and 30 minutes for baking.

For plain pastry (two crust pastry):

Flour	2 cups	Salt	1 tsp
Butter	2/3 cups	Water chilled	5 to 6 tbsp

For stuffing:

Kidney beans boiled	2 cups	Minced meat	400 gm
Or soya granules	1 cup	Tomatoes roasted and chopped	2 large
Onion chopped fine	1 no.	Mushrooms sliced	½ cup
Capsicum chopped	¼ cup	Red pepper chopped	2 tbsp.
Basil chopped	2 tsp	Cheese grated	½ cup

Adobo sauce	2 tbsp	Butter	2 tbsp.
Salt & pepper	to taste	Cilantro chopped	¼ cup

Preparation for stuffing:

1. Brown the mushrooms and capsicums in butter and lift out.
2. In the same pan, put onion and cook till golden; add minced meat and fry for 5 minutes. Add tomatoes and adobo; cook further for 2 to 3 minutes. Add salt, pepper, and basil. Sprinkle ½ cup water over it; stir; cover and cook for 7 minutes or till mince is cooked.
3. Or soak Soya granules in warm water for 1 hour; drain and discard water; squeeze the granules well and use in place of minced meat. To squeeze water from granules, place them on a clean napkin, wrap it like a toffee, hold from both ends and squeeze with both the hands. Rest, follow the recipe completely.
4. Mix boiled beans, cheese and cilantro. Stir properly, cover and keep aside.

Preparation for pastry:

1. Sieve flour and salt together. Add butter to flour and mix it with your fingertips till the flour resembles bread crumbs.
2. Now add cold water to hold ingredients together. Sprinkle a little more cold water evenly and form a ball. Divide the mixture into two portions.
3. Roll out one portion in a circular shape on lightly floured board.
4. It should be about 1/8 - inch thick. Fit loosely into 8" or 9" pie shell. Gently pat out air pockets. Trim pastry to 1" of edge of pie pan/shell, fold underneath. Roll out the second portion also in the same way. Fill the pastry with the filling. Cut slits in the second circle of pastry to allow steam to escape; place over filling; fold edge of top pastry under lower pastry to form a standing rim.
6. Pinch pastry edges or press with fork.
7. Bake it in moderately hot oven for 25 to 30 minutes.

Serving: Serve the baked pie hot as a main meal with some light soup.

Tips: Soya products are as healthy as meat products are. Soya protein is a high quality protein, hence, a good replacement for vegetarians.

26. Garlic-flavoured Lemon Beans

You Require: **Cooking Time:** 15 minutes.

French/butter beans	200 gm	Fried onion slices	¼ cup
Garlic slivers	2 tbsp	Or olive oil	2 tbsp
Or Butter	2 tbsp	Lemons	2 to 3 nos.
Salt	to taste	Coriander/parsley chopped	¼ cup

Preparation and Cooking:

1. Wash and string the beans; cut them into desirable size and steam for 4 minutes in a microwave. To avoid discolouration remove them immediately and place under running water. Keep them in a strainer.
2. Or boil the beans with 1and ½ cup water and a pinch of salt in it, on high fire. Rinse under running water and keep them aside.
3. Squeeze 1 and ½ lemons; slice other half and keep aside to serve with.
4. Heat oil or butter and fry garlic slivers in it; add peppercorns and beans; stir to coat well; sprinkle salt and lemon juice; stir once again and add chopped coriander or parsley. Remove from the fire.

Serving: Garnish the beans with fried onion slices; place the sliced lemon on the side and serve hot as a side dish with any meal.

27. Burritos

Burritos are flour tortillas rolled with a filling inside and served warm.

You Require: **Cooking Time:** 35 to 40 minutes if flour

Large flour or wheat tortillas 6 to 8 no (tortillas are cooked in advance)

Vegetarian/non-vegetarian filling	3 cups	Red sauce to serve with	2 cups
Simple white rice	2 cups	Cheese grated	1 cup or more
Pickled vegetables chopped fine	1 cup	Or jalapeno chopped	1 cup

How to make vegetarian filling:

Soya granules	1 to 1 and ½ cup	Onion chopped	1 no.
Or Boiled kidney beans		Garlic chopped	2 tbsp
Oregano dried	1 tsp	Chilli sauce	1 tbsp
Tomato puree	¼ cup	Green chilli deseeded and chopped	1 no.
Coriander/parsley chopped	3 tbsp	Olive oil/butter	3 tbsp
Salt	to taste	Corn flour	2 tbsp mixed in 4 tbsp water
Roasted sesame seeds	2 tbsp (opt)		

Preparation and Cooking:

1. Soak soya granules in warm water for 30 minutes; drain water and squeeze the granules properly. Keep aside.
2. Chop pickled vegetables very fine.
3. Heat fat in the pan and add chopped chilli, garlic and onion and cook till translucent. Add soya granules and cook stirring for 2 minutes.
4. Add chilli and tomato sauces, oregano and salt; cook for 1 minute and add ½ cup water;

cover and cook on medium fire till water is dried up. Add corn flour and mix; cook for a few seconds till the mixture appears homogeneous and switch off the heat.

5. Sprinkle coriander.

Note: Instead of soya granules use kidney beans and follow rest of the recipe.

For non-vegetarian filling:

Cooked and shredded chicken	3 cups	Onion chopped	1 no.
Garlic chopped	2 tbsp	Butter/olive oil	3 tbsp
Oregano dried	1 tsp	Chilli sauce	1 tbsp
Tomato puree	¼ cup	Green chilli deseeded and chopped	1 no.
Coriander/parsley chopped	3 tbsp	Salt	to taste

Preparation and Cooking:

1. Heat fat in the pan and add chopped chilli, garlic and onion and cook till translucent. Add chicken and cook stirring for 2 minutes or till well coated.
2. Add chilli and tomato sauces, oregano and salt; cook for 1 minute and add ½ cup water; cover and cook on medium fire till water is dried up. Add corn flour and mix; cook for a few seconds and switch off the heat.
3. Sprinkle coriander.

For Red sauce: The recipe has been written in 'Prawns in Red Sauce'.

Assembling of Burritos:

1. To assemble place 1 tortilla on the working platform; place 3 to 4 tbsp filling on it, 1-inch away from one end; sprinkle grated cheese generously over it; sprinkle 2 tbsp rice and finally top it with 2 tbsp pickled vegetables or a little jalepeno.
2. Fold the left end over it and roll forward to give it a proper shape. Fold all the burritos like this and place either in the microwave or in preheated oven.
3. If you want to heat Burritos in a microwave, then cover them loosely with 2 layers of paper napkins and heat on REHEAT mode for a couple of minutes. And if you place them in a preheated oven, then give 10 to 15 minutes or till heated through but not crisp.

Serving: Garnish with red sauce and serve Burritos hot as a main meal with other accompaniments, such as a soup or a beverage, for lunch or dinner.

Tips: Many people like burritos shallow fried till crisp; so, after filling and rolling shallow fry burritos and serve.

28. Chicken with Pistachio Nuts Sauce

(Pollo en Pistachio Mole)

It is a delicious festival dish for gourmets which can be cooked to celebrate other important events of life as well.

You require:		**Cooking Time:** About 1 hour and 15 minutes.	
Chicken breast	4 nos.	Salt	1 tsp
Lemon-juice	3 tbsp	Cloves	4 nos.
Cinnamon stick	1 inch piece	Dry chillies whole	2 nos.
All spice berries	8 nos.	Peppercorns	12 no
Sesame seeds	¼ cup	Oil	for frying
Cornmeal or breadcrumbs	½ cup	Eggs	2 nos.

For Pistachio Nuts Sauce:

Pistachio nuts	½ cup shelled	Green chillies	3 nos.
Sesame seeds	¼ cup	Garlic chopped	2 tbsp
Anise seed	¼ tsp	Salt	to taste
Cilantro chopped	¼ cup	Chicken broth	2 cups + water 1 cup
		Or Chicken stock	3 to 4 cups

Preparation and Cooking:

1. Dry roast dried chillies, peppercorn, all spiceberries, cinnamon and cloves in a heavy based pan on medium fire for 5 minutes or so. Cool and powder in a mixer.
   Or place all the spices in an envelope; place it in a microwave and cook on micro HIGH for 1 and ½ minute. Shake the envelope after 1 minute in between. Cool and powder the spices.
2. Flatten the chicken breasts with a meat flattener. Mix the powdered spices with lemon juice and salt; rub the chicken breasts with it and keep marinated for 4 hours or overnight under refrigeration.
3. Meantime, make pistachio nuts sauce.
4. Deseed green chillies and chop roughly.
5. Combine pistachio nuts, sesame seeds, aniseeds, garlic, chilli, cilantro and half of chicken broth or stock in a blender and blend well. Pour into a pan and mix rest of the stock; cook on medium heat for 30 to 35 minutes or till sauce is slightly thickened and shiny in appearance. It should coat the spoon if tested.
6. Check the seasonings; cover and keep it warm.
7. Combine cornmeal and sesame seeds in a plate. Beat eggs. Drain chicken breasts; save the liquid; strain and mix with sauce. Lift the chicken breasts one by one; dip in the beaten egg and roll in the cornmeal mixture thoroughly. Keep aside for 15 minutes.
8. Meanwhile, heat oil in a frying pan/kadai and deep fry chicken in it from both the sides; drain on a kitchen paper.

Serving: Pour pistachio nuts sauce in a shallow serving dish; place fried chicken on top;

garnish with pickled jalapeno slices and serve the dish hot with flour Tortillas and simple White rice.

Variation: Serve fried/roasted fish or roasted meats with Pistachio nuts sauce. Vegetarians can use paneer instead of chicken and follow rest of the recipe.

Tips: Sauce can be cooked in advance; covered and stored under refrigeration. Warm it up in a microwave on REHEAT mode or on slow fire before use.

If you want to make sauce for vegetarian preparation, use taste making vegetarian soup cube dissolved in measured liquid (veg-stock or water) and use in stead of chicken broth.

29. Peanut Crusted Fish with Pineapple Sauce

This aw-some dish is based on innovative instincts of such chefs who within the frame work of traditions keep experimenting with the available food ingredients to bring out the excellence in food and taste.

You Require: **Cooking Time:** 1 hour to 1 and ½ hour.

Halibut or any other good fish400 fillets (100 to 150 gm each)

For peanut crust:

Chilli peanuts	¾ cup	Garlic	6 cloves
Oregano dried	½ tsp	Chilli powder	¼ tsp
Peppercorns	¼ tsp	Scallions/shallots	¼ cup
Cilantro/coriander chopped	¼ cup	(trimmed and chopped)	
Egg	1 no.	All purpose flour	2 tbsp
Oil for frying			

For Pineapple sauce:

Pineapple diced	2 cup	Orange juice	½ cup
Red chillies (dry) toasted and seeded	12 nos.	Garlic	10 cloves
Mexican cinnamon	1 and ½ inch piece	Salt	to taste
Cumin powder	¾ tsp	Clove powder	¼ tsp
Olive oil	3 tbsp	Water	1 cup
Sugar	1 tbsp	Wine vinegar	1 tbsp

Preparation and Cooking:

1. Soak red chillies in warm water for 20 to 30 minutes.
2. Roast garlic and peel.
3. **Make peanut crust mixture.** Combine chilli peanuts, garlic, oregano, peppercorns, chilli powder, scallions and cilantro in a blender/food processor. Process using on and off quick pulses until the peanuts are finely chopped.

4. **Make pineapple sauce:** Drain the soaked chillies and combine with diced pineapple, orange juice, garlic, cinnamon, cumin and clove powders and water in a blender jar and blend until very smooth. Add ¼ cup more water in a blender if needed be.

   Note: Uncooked blended sauce can be used to marinate meat, fish or poultry.
5. Heat olive oil in a heavy based pan over medium heat; pour in the blended sauce and bring it to the boiling point; simmer the sauce stirring in between until the sauce is shiny and has thickened.
6. If the sauce thickens before taking a nice sheen, add up to 1 cup more water and continue cooking. Add water, only a few spoons at a time. It will take 30 to 35 minutes for sauce to cook. Now stir in the sugar, salt and vinegar. Mix well.
7. Strain the sauce through a fine sieve, pushing down the residues in the sieve to get as much sauce out of them as possible. Check the seasonings. Cover and keep the sauce warm.
8. Preheat the oven for moderate heat.
9. Spread peanut crust mixture in a plate.
10. Dredge the fish with all purpose flour; beat egg with a pinch of salt; dip the one side of the fish in the beaten egg, let the extra egg drop back in the bowl; press the egged side of the fish fillet into the crust mixture, pressing gently to get as much of the topping to stick as possible. Keep the coated side of the fillet up on a plate. Repeat the process with rest of the remaining fillets.
11. Heat oil in a pan on medium high flame; add the fish fillets topping side up and cook until the undersides are golden brown; spoon hot oil over the topping occasionally, and it will take about 4 to 5 minutes before the fillets are cooked.
12. Transfer the fillets to a baking dish and place it in the hot oven for 10 to 15 minutes until the topping of the fish is lightly browned and it feels firm to touch.
13. Meanwhile, heat up sauce either reheating in a microwave or simmering it on low heat. Thin it by adding a few drops of water to restore the right consistency if needed be.

Serving: Put ¼ cup sauce onto each serving plate and top it with fish fillet. Garnish with lemon wedges and serve immediately with flour tortillas or plain rice.

Tips: Pineapple sauce can be prepared a couple of days in advance and stored in the coolest part of your refrigerator. Take it out 30 minutes before use and reheat when fish is being cooked in oven.

30. Mexican Style Pasta with Meat Sauce and Olives

You Require: **Cooking Time:** 1 hour or so.

Minced meat	300 gm	Capsicum	1 nos. small
Onion	1 no. medium	Garlic clove	1 no.
Cooking oil	3 tbsp	Red chilli powder	1 tsp

Basil dry	½ tsp	Tomato puree	½ cup
Tomato chopped (roasted and skinned)	1 medium		
Dry Red wine	¼ cup	Stock cube (chicken)	1 no.
Butter	1 tbsp	Coriander chopped	2 tbsp
Any pasta	150 gm	Green olives	8 to 10 nos.
Salt and pepper	to taste		

Preparation and Cooking:

1. Peel and chop onion and garlic very fine.
2. Chop capsicum and slice olives.
3. Heat oil in a pan and sauté onion and garlic till onion is transparent. Add capsicum and cook for a few seconds.
4. Add meat to the pan and brown well; stir in chilli powder, basil, salt and pepper; cook stirring for 1 minute.
5. Now add tomato puree, red wine, stock cube and chopped tomato. Mix properly.
6. Cover and cook for 30 to 35 minutes or till meat is done. Stir in between and add ¼ to ½ cup water if the mixture becomes too dry.
7. Boil pasta with in a large pan with ½ tsp salt and drain well; place the pasta in a serving dish and dot it with butter.
8. Sprinkle chopped coriander over the cooked meat sauce and mix in half the sliced olives.

Serving: Pour the sauce over boiled pasta and garnish it with remaining olives. Serve the dish hot as part of the main meal or as a light lunch.

Tips: Meat sauce can be prepared a day in advance and pasta can be boiled one hour before serving.

31. Green, Red and Yellow Peppers Stuffed

You Require: **Cooking Time:** 1 hour.

Red peppers	2 nos. small	Green peppers	2 nos. small
Yellow peppers	2 nos. small	Boiled rice or Simple white rice	2 cups
Garlic chopped fine	1 tbsp	Cheese grated	½ cup
Mutton minced cooked	1 cup	Cooking oil	2 tbsp
Or Any other left over meat shredded		Seasonings	to taste
Parsley chopped	¼ cup		

Preparation and Cooking:

1. Wash and dry peppers with kitchen towel. With a sharp knife remove the tops and clean inside without damaging the shells. Brush the shells with a little oil from outside and keep aside.

2. Chop the pepper flesh removed from the tops fine, discarding the stems.
3. Preheat the oven.
4. Heat oil in a pan; fry garlic till pinkish in colour; add rice and fry for a while; mix cooked mince/meat and season it according to your taste. Remove from the fire, add half the grated cheese and chopped parsley and mix gently.
5. Stuff the peppers with this mixture; sprinkle cheese on the top generously.

Bake them in hot oven for 35 to 40 minutes.

Serving: Serve the peppers hot with bread and a soup as a meal. They can also be served at room temperature.

Tips: You may bake single coloured peppers.

Stuff for filling peppers can vary, any veg or non-veg - rice based or meat based mixture can be used. Even leftover meats can be shredded and mixed with rice or vegetables.

Seasonings can also vary. You may use chilli powder or paste, black pepper powder, oregano, all spice or cinnamon powder etc.

32. Pescado-Maiz Cakes

(Fancy Fish and Corn Cakes)

You Require: **Cooking Time:** 40 to 45 minutes.

Corn on cobs	3 nos.	Boiled fish flakes	3 cups
Fresh bread crumbs	1 cup	Onion chopped	1 no. small
Green chillies chopped	2 to 3 nos.	Mixed spice powder	1 tsp
Red chilli powder	1 tsp	Egg	1 no.
Corn meal	¼ cup	Coriander chopped	¼ cup
Salt and pepper	to taste	Green and Red Salsa to serve with	
Oil for frying			

Preparation and Cooking:

1. Grate corn on cobs.
2. Mash fish flakes with your hands.
3. In a large working bowl or trove combine together grated corn, mashed fish and all other ingredients except oil for frying.
4. Mash the mixture well with your hands and divide into 12 to 16 balls.
5. Flatten the balls and shape them in any fancy form, or just flatten the balls and cook. You may either deep fry the corn cakes or shallow fry them in a heavy bottomed pan to a golden brown colour. Drain them on kitchen oil absorbent paper and serve them hot.

Serving: Serve the Fish and Corn cakes hot with salsas as a snack or with soup and salad as a light meal.

Tips: You may steam fish with centre bone either in a microwave for 5 to 6 minutes on High or on gas stove heat; cool and remove the skin and bones.

To get the fresh breadcrumbs, place the pieces of fresh bread slices in an electric grinder and churn for a while.

33. Courgette Mexican

Courgettes are one of the favourite vegetables of Mexicans. This simple dish is popularly prepared in their households. It is not only low in calories but also a good source of vitamin C. The combination of pines and cottage cheese makes it a balanced dish for vegetarians.

You Require: **Cooking Time:** 30 to 35 minutes.

Zucchini/courgettes	3 no.	Pine nuts	¼ cup
Salt-n-pepper	to taste	Chilli flakes	1 tsp (opt)
Cottage cheese	½ cup (opt)	Cooking oil for shallow frying	

Preparation and Cooking:

1. Slice courgettes/zucchini diagonally.
2. Heat oil in a pan and shallow fry the slices from both sides. Drain them on kitchen paper.
3. Or brush the slices with olive oil from both sides and grill them for 10 to 15 minutes, changing the side once.
4. Arrange them in a plate and sprinkle salt and pepper evenly.
5. Crumble cottage cheese and spread over courgette slices. Season it if you like. Sprinkle a few chilli flakes over it.

Serving: Garnish the dish with pine nuts and serve it immediately as a side dish.

Variation: Spread any other mixture over shallow fried courgettes and garnish with chopped cilantro/parsley.

34. Roasted Eggplant and Corn Bake

Vegetarians' favourite, this dish is a meal in itself.

You Require: **Cooking Time:** 1 hour.

Corn kernels	2 cups	Eggplant	1 no. medium
Eggs	2 to 3 no.	Sour cream	1 cup
Tomato puree	2 tbsp (opt)	Butter	3 tbsp
Cheese grated	½ cup	Jalapenos	3 no.
Garlic crushed	1 tsp	Oregano dry	1 tsp
Pepper powder	½ tsp	Chilli powder	¼ tsp
Salt	to taste		

Preparation and Cooking:

1. Cut eggplant into 1-inch squares; sprinkle 1 tsp salt, mix and keep aside for 1 hour to remove the bitter juices. Then strain through a colander.
2. Roast and peel jalapenos; deseed and cut into small pieces.
3. Preheat oven for moderate heat.
4. Melt 2 tbsp butter and smear eggplant pieces with it; place the pieces in a baking tray and bake for 20 minutes and remove. Or deep fry the eggplant pieces and drain on kitchen paper. Do not switch off the oven.
5. Meantime, place eggs, corn, sour cream, tomato puree if using and remaining butter, and blend well. Pour the contents into a large bowl; add grated cheese, salt, pepper, garlic and jalapeno pieces and mix.
6. Grease an ovenproof dish with butter and layer it with roasted eggplant pieces; pour the egg- cream mixture over it; shake the dish lightly and sprinkle it with oregano and chilli powder.
7. Bake in hot oven for 35 to 40 minutes or till the dish is nicely set. Stand it for 10 minutes.

Serving: Serve it hot as a main dish with any soup/stew and melba toast or garlic bread.

Variation: Add 1 cup diced and boiled ham to the mixture before baking.

Or instead of corn use chicken or mutton mince; cook it for 5 minutes in a non stick pan and combine with eggplant and egg mixture. Rest, bake the dish in the same way as explained above.

35. Budin

(Tortilla Gratin with Cilantro Sauce)

Budine's literal meaning is a pudding. Budines can be composed of just about anything. They are usually the home dishes which can be prepared like lasagnas. They can be prepared with left over tortillas, shredded chicken or meats, or combination of vegetables, then moistened with a variety of sauces and finally baked.

You Require: **Cooking Time:** 1 hour.

Tortillas corn or flour	2 to 3 nos.	Oil	for frying
Chicken shredded	3 cups		
Or Combination of partly cooked veggies 3 cup			
Butter	2 tbsp	Onion chopped	1 no.
Garlic chopped	1 tbsp	Flour	2 tbsp
Chicken stock	3 cups	Cheese grated	½ cup
Potato boiled	1 no. small	Tomato seeded and sliced	1 no.
Chillies green chopped	2 nos.	Coriander chopped	1 cup
Oregano dry	1 tsp	Pickled jalapenos	4 to 5 nos.
Olives	6 nos.	Salt-n-pepper	to taste
Fresh cream	¼ cup (opt)		

Preparation and Cooking:

1. Cut tortillas into ½-inch strips and deep fry till crisp, remove from oil and place on kitchen paper. Or brush tortillas, cut them into strips and crisp them in a hot oven.
2. Slice jalapenos and olives and keep aside.
3. Make cilantro sauce. Heat butter in a pan and sauté onion and garlic; add green chillies and stir, add flour and fry till golden; add coriander and fry for a while; put potato and chicken stock, and simmer for 5 minutes. Switch off the heat. Cool the mixture; pass through a blender and sieve.
4. Season it with salt, pepper and oregano. Mix in half the grated cheese and cream.
5. Grease a baking dish; spread 1 cup sauce in it; arrange crisp tortilla strips over it; place shredded chicken/steamed vegetables and sliced jalapenos and cover them with the remaining sauce; arrange sliced olives and tomato wedges and sprinkle remaining cheese on top.
6. Bake in a hot oven for 30 to 35 minutes till the sauce starts bubbling and top is golden brown. Switch off the heat. Stand the dish for 5 minutes in the oven.

Serving: Serve it hot with tomato sauce and a soup or a salad.

Tips: The number of tortillas used in the recipe is determined by the size of tortillas.

36. Green Beans Omelette

Fresh green beans, low in calories and rich in nutrients fall in the category of a good dietary fibre. Omelette stuffed with steamed beans and served with warm tortillas/crusty bread makes a nutritious breakfast meal.

You Require: **Cooking Time:** 5 to 7 minutes for each omelette.

Eggs large	8 nos.		
Green beans steamed & chopped fine	1 cup		
Unsalted butter or cooking oil	2 tbsp	Freshly ground black pepper	to taste
Salt	to taste	Parsley/coriander chopped	¼ cup
Grated cheese	4 tbsp (opt)	Chilli-garlic sauce	as per requirement
Tortillas/bread to serve	2 to 3 nos.		

Preparation and Cooking:

1. Break and beat 2 eggs at a time in a bowl until frothy and season with salt and pepper.
2. Heat a non-stick pan on medium fire and smear it with ½ tbsp butter/cooking oil.
3. Pour in the beaten eggs and cook, gently stirring with a wooden spatula till the eggs are almost set. Sprinkle over ¼-th portion of beans and 1 tbsp grated cheese; fold it gently and transfer to the serving plate.
4. Spoon some of the sauce on top and serve it hot.

Serving: Serve the dish hot garnished with parsley and warm tortillas or bread to be enjoyed with at breakfast.

Or serve it at any other meal with a soup and fresh salad

Information: While making an omelette stirring the eggs helps to break down their protein and making them easier to digest. Bottom of the omelette should not burn, otherwise after consuming it causes acidity.

37. Poached Eggs in Tomato Sauce

Eggs an excellent source of high protein, vitamins and minerals are just ideal for any meal, particularly for people those are vegetarian by nature but enjoy eggs in any form.

You Require: **Cooking Time:** 30 to 35 minutes.

Eggs	8 nos.

For sauce:

Tomatoes	1000 gm	Onion chopped	1 large
Garlic chopped	4 to 5 cloves	Bay leaf	1 no.
Water/stock	3 and ½ cups	Green chillies roasted	3 nos.
Olive/cooking oil	2 tbsp	Salt and pepper	to taste
Coriander chopped	3 tbsp	Mozzarella cheese	60 gm
Corn tortillas to serve	8 to 10 nos.		

Preparation and Cooking:

1. Cut roasted chillies into strips.
2. Cut mozzarella cheese into juliennes.
3. Chop tomatoes roughly and place in a blender; add chopped onions, garlic and half of the water and blend to a smooth mixture. Add rest of the stock and pass the tomato mixture through a sieve.
4. Heat oil in a heavy bottomed pan over a medium heat and add tomato mixture in it. Drop in a bay leaf and cook for 15 to 20 minutes on medium fire, stirring occasionally. Add the chilli strips. If sauce happens to be very thick, heat ½ cup stock or water and add to the sauce. Bring it to the boil and season the sauce with salt and pepper.
5. Pour the sauce in a shallow heat proof dish or a pan with a lid.
6. Break in the eggs one by one; cover and cook over low heat for a few minutes until the whites of the eggs are set.
7. Or place the dish in a moderately hot oven and cook till the whites are set. Just before removing the dish from the heat, add mozzarella juliennes.

Serving: Garnish the eggs with coriander and serve hot immediately accompanied by warm tortillas.

38. Mole Poblano de Pollo

(Chocolate Chicken)

Spaniards call a sauce 'mole'. It is believed that it originated in Pubela. Originally, this pubelan speciality was known as 'mole de olor', a mole of fragrance and aroma. "When you say mole poblano, nonnatives immediately think of 'chocolate chicken', and natives' mouths water to visions of a dark, complex sauce made of dried chillies, nuts, seeds, flavouring vegetables, spices and yes, a bit of chocolate", says Rick Bayless in his book 'Authentic Mexican'. It is one of the most famous Mexican dishes. This complex sauce is made of various flavours. It is prepared with a variety of chillies, nuts, seeds, herbs, spices and a bit of chocolate,.it is believed that the flavours of this mole begin to fuse during cooking but a day later the fusion is complete. Beside other ingredients, Mexicans use the variety of chillies such as mulatos, anchos, pasilla and chipotle for this dish but here we have used easily available Indian Kashmiri chillies, roasted and seeded.

You Require: **Cooking Time:** 1 and ½hour.

Chicken	1 no./800 to 900 gm	Dried red chillies (deseeded)	6 nos.
Almonds	2 tbsp	Sesame seeds	2 tbsp + 1 tsp
Raisins	3 tbsp	Coriander seeds	1 tsp
Cooking oil	¼ cup or more	Onion sliced	1 medium
Tomato	1 large	Garlic peeled	2 cloves
Dry bread	2 slices	Pepper powder	¼ tsp
Clove powder	a pinch	Aniseeds	½ tsp
Cinnamon powder	1 tsp	Sugar	2 tsp
Salt	to taste	Stock/water	1 and ½ cup
Chocolate	2" piece		

Preparation and Cooking:

1. Cut chicken into 8 pieces or buy the precut chicken. Dry with kitchen towel and set aside.
2. Roughly chop tomatoes and put in a bowl, and chop chocolate and add to it.
3. Place a pan over the medium heat and dry roast the sesame and coriander seeds till lightly browned. Take out 1 tsp roasted sesame seeds for garnishing. Put them in the bowl containing tomatoes.
4. Heat oil in a pan and fry the deseeded red chillies till nut brown in colour; lower the heat; remove chillies from oil and place them in a bowl; cover them with hot water, place a lid and stand submerged for 1 hour.
5. In the same oil, fry almonds and remove. Add raisins and fry for a few seconds or till they are puff and brown. Mix almonds and raisins with tomato mixture.
6. Fry onion and garlic till well browned, drain and mix with tomatoes. Break bread into pieces and fry too. Add to the tomatoes.

7. Pour a little more oil in the same pan and fry chicken pieces in it. Remove and keep them aside covered.
8. Place the tomato mixture in an electric blender, add 1-cup stock and blend well or till the mixture is smooth. Remove the mixture and puree the soaked chillies.
9. Now fry first the chilli puree in the same oil till thick and dark; add the onion, tomato and nut puree and fry well until thick once again. Pour rest of the stock and ½ to 1 cup water and simmer the sauce for 30 minutes on medium heat. At this point add rest of the dry spices and seasonings. Check the seasonings.
10. When the mole is cooking, preheat the oven. Arrange chicken pieces in an ovenproof dish, large enough to hold chicken and sauce. Pour the sauce over chicken; cover the dish with a foil and bake it for 50 minutes to 1 hour.
11. Check the doneness of meat.

Serving: Sprinkle the toasted sesame over the dish before serving and serve this speciality with white or green Mexican rice or tortillas.

39. Stuffed Chillies in Ranchera Sauce

Chillies are eaten in Mexico in many forms. Stuffed chillies fried in a batter, stuffed and charred chillies are not uncommon sights on a Mexican table.

Big chillies first roasted, peeled and stuffed with vegetables or minced meats; placed in Ranchera sauce and finally baked, makes an excellent side dish.

You Require: **Cooking Time:** 35 minutes

Big chillies green/red	6 to 8 nos.	Well flavoured veg/non-veg stuffing	1 cup
Ranchera sauce	1 cup	Parsley chopped	1 tbsp

Preparation and Cooking:

1. Roast chillies directly on naked fire one by one, turning frequently with a kitchen tong and place them in a plastic bag for 20 minutes. Remove from the bag and scrape all the burnt skin with a knife. Clean with a wet napkin. Carefully slit the chillies and deseed them. Discard the seeds.
2. Stuff all the chillies with the filling of your choice.
3. Pour Ranchera sauce in a shallow micro safe dish and place the chillies in it.
4. Cover the dish with cling wrap and cook in a microwave for 5 minutes on HIGH. Remove the wrap from the dish just before serving.
5. Or Pour the sauce in an oven-proof shallow dish and place the stuffed chillies in it. Cover the dish with aluminium foil and cook in moderately preheated oven for 30 to 35 minutes. Un cover the dish just before serving it.

Serving: Sprinkle the chopped parsley on top and serve it as a side dish.

Tips: Chillies can be stuffed, covered and stored under refrigeration much in advance and the last step cooking can be done before serving it.

40. Baked Eggs-n-Spinach

Eggs are one of the most important ingredients of Mexican meals. They are cooked in number of ways. Cooking eggs in Ranchera sauce is traditional and are eaten at breakfast with a variety of breads. Here the dish is cooked in an innovative way with spinach puree which is equally healthy, nutritious and colourful.

You Require: **Cooking Time:** 40 to 45 minutes.

Spinach puree	2 cups	Cream	¼ to ½ cup
Onion chopped	1 small	Garlic chopped	1 tbsp
Green chilli paste	1 tbsp	Butter	1 tbsp
Or pepper powder	1 tsp/to taste	Cumin powder	½ tsp
Clove powder	¼ tsp	Salt	to taste
Eggs	4 to 6 nos.		

Preparation and Cooking:

1. Preheat an oven to 180 degrees Celsius.
2. Grease an oven-proof dish.
3. Heat butter in a non-stick pan and sauté onion and garlic in it. Add chilli paste and fry for a second or two. Add spinach puree and cook till no liquid is left. Season it with salt and cumin-n-clove powders. Mix cream and transfer the spinach to the oven-proof dish.
4. Make depressions in the spinach with the back of a table/serving spoon. Break one egg each in one depression and sprinkle a little salt over the eggs.
5. Place the dish in the hot oven for 25 to 30 minutes or till the white part of the eggs sets well and spinach is nicely heated through. Switch off the oven and let the dish stand for 5 minutes before serving.

Serving: Serve the dish hot with Garlic bread/Tortillas.

Mexican 'Carrot and Beetroot Soup' is a good accompaniment to this dish if served for a main meal.

Variations: Instead of cream, add some cheese in the spinach and add no salt at all.

Instead of spinach mixture, use **Ranchera sauce** and follow the rest of the process from step no 4 of the cooking.

Desserts

Exquisite Mango Sorbet, 136

Almond and Cinnamon Cookies, 132

Baked Creamy Rice Pudding, 133

Caramalized Bananas, 136

Caramel Custard, 141

Chocolate Coffee Mousse, 137

Chocolate Sorbet, 140

Watermelon Ice, 139

Mixed Melons Delight, 131

Raspberry Ice Cream, 138

Tender Hearts, 134

Walnut Dessert, 131

Chocolate-chilli Cake, 143

Desserts

Traditionally, Mexicans use a variety of fruits for desserts. Either they serve fruits as such in an interesting way or they are turned into unusual ice-creams, ices and sorbets. Chocolate or cocoa is used a lot for creating a variety of cakes, soufflés or mousses. Flavoured cream or fruit-based sauces are prepared to serve the cakes and cookies with.

1. Mixed Melon Delight

Refreshing and soothing melon starter or dessert is not only ideal for hot summer months, but aesthetically too this nutritious dish appeals to the senses and satiates the diner.

You Require: **Preparation Time:** 30 minutes.

Water melon	1 medium size	Melons	2 nos.
Lemon-juice	2 tbsp	Castor sugar	2 tbsp (opt)
Melon ball scooper			

Preparation:

1. Cut melons into halves and take out as many balls with a scooper as you can. Place them in a container with a lid; sprinkle lemon juice; cover and chill.
2. Or cut them into equal-sized pieces and follow the procedure.
3. Sprinkle castor sugar and mix lightly.

Serving: Serve the mixed melon balls or cubes on skewers or serve them in individual small bowls with fruit forks either as a starter or as a dessert.

You may garnish the dish with fresh basil or mint leaves.

Tips: It is ideal if you could use red balls/cubes of water-melon and green and orange-coloured cubes/balls from melons for this dish.

2. Walnut Dessert

This is one of the firm and soft desserts made in Mexico. Mostly, such sweets are prepared with milk, sugar and nuts, such as walnuts, almonds, pine nuts, pumpkin seeds and strawberries, etc., and are cooked on slow fire and are known as **Jamoncillo.** This particular dessert, 'walnut jamoncillo' is one of the sweets made for festivities.

You Require: **Cooking Time:** 40 to 45 minutes.

Walnuts shelled	250 gm	Egg	1 large
Granulated sugar	100 gm	Milk	100 ml

Preparation and Cooking:

1. Ground walnuts, saving a few for garnishing. Chop the saved ones and keep aside.
2. Beat the egg and place in a heavy-based pan/kadai.
3. Add ground walnuts, sugar and milk and mix thoroughly.
4. Cook over medium heat, stirring constantly for 25 to 30 minutes till it is a homogeneous mass and you can see the base of the pan.
5. Remove from the heat and continue stirring for a few more minutes until it starts setting.
6. Transfer the mixture to a shallow square or rectangular dish-/-tray; and leave it to cool thoroughly
7. When solid, cut into approximately 1-inch cubes.

Serving: Decorate the cubes with chopped walnuts and serve.

Tips: This dish is nearer to Indian Chikki or any fudge preparation which is made with various ingredients and just ideal for cold weather. As we all know that the walnuts are a good source of protein, iron and calcium, and such desserts give instant energy to the tired body.

No doubt, this is one of the festive dishes but otherwise also such desserts give instant energy to the tired body.

3. Almond and Cinnamon Cookies

(Galletas De Almendra Y Ganela)

You Require: **Cooking Time:** 10 to 12 minutes for baking

All purpose flour	1 and ½ cup	Butter	125 gm
Almonds (not toasted)	¾ cup	Sugar	½ cup
Brown sugar	¼ to ½ cup	Egg	1 no.
Egg yolk	1 no.	Cinnamon powder	½ tsp
Baking powder	½ tsp	Baking soda	¼ tsp
Vanilla essence	½ tsp	Salt	a pinch

Preparation and Cooking:

1. Sliver almonds and keep aside.
2. Sift together flour, cinnamon powder, salt, baking soda and baking powder into a bowl.
3. In a large bowl, with a rotary beater (hand or electric), beat butter and both the sugars together till fluffy; add egg and egg yolks and beat thoroughly. Add vanilla essence and beat once again.
4. Add the dry ingredients and slivered almonds and mix at slow speed until well mixed.
5. Divide the dough into 2 equal parts; roll each one into a log about 10 inches long; wrap each log separately in 2 layers of plastic sheets and freeze the logs for at least 4 hours._

   Note: The dough can be frozen up to 2 months.

6. Preheat the oven to moderate heat.
7. Cut the log or logs into ¼-inch thick slices; place the cookies on ungreased baking trays with at least 1-inch gap between them.
8. Bake them for 10 to 12 minutes or until golden brown around the edges.
9. Cool the cookies in the baking sheets for 5 minutes; then using a spatula or palate knife, transfer them on the wire rack for cooling completely.
10. Once cool, store them in an air-tight container up to 4 to 5 days.

Serving: Serve fresh cookies at the tea time or as a dessert accompanied with cinnamon sauce.

Cooking time: Baking time is 10 to 12 minutes, whereas preparation time is more.

4. Baked Creamy Rice Pudding

An easy-to-make baked rice pudding in Mexican style that is light for stomach too.

You Require: **Cooking Time:** 45 minutes to 1 hour.

Rice	½ cup	Milk	3 cups
Powder milk	¼ cup	Sugar	½ cup
Eggs	2 nos.	Cinnamon stick	2"inch long piece
Raisins cleaned and washed	¼ cup	Lemon rind	1 tsp
Butter	1 tbsp	Cinnamon powder	for garnishing

Preparation and Cooking:

1. Wash rice thoroughly in running water; combine with 1 cup water and cook till soft, stirring several times.
2. Add milk and cinnamon stick; bring the mixture to the boiling point and reduce the heat, cook rice and milk for 30 minutes on medium fire or till creamy.
3. Add sugar, powder milk and egg yolks. Mix thoroughly with a wooden spoon and remove from fire after couple of minutes. Slightly cool it. Remove the cinnamon stick and discard. Add lemon rind and mix.
4. Heat oven for a moderate heat.
5. Grease an oven-proof dish with melted butter.
6. Beat egg whites thoroughly till stiff and gently fold into the creamy rice-milk mixture. Throw in the raisins and stir.
7. Pour the mixture in the greased dish and bake for 15 to 20 minutes or till the top of the pudding is just golden pale.

Serving: Garnish the hot pudding with cinnamon powder and serve it hot or at room temperature.

Or cool it, cover it with aluminium foil or cling wrap and chill it before serving.

5. Peanut-Chocolate Cake with Caramel Custard

You Require: **Cooking Time:** 50 minutes.

Peanuts roasted and crushed	1 cup	Eggs	2 nos.
Flour	1 ½ cup	Butter melted	½ cup
Coco powder	½ cup leveled	Unsweetened chocolate	1/3 cup
Sugar	1¼ cup	Baking powder	½tsp
Baking soda	1 tsp	Milk	¾ cup or more

Preparation and Cooking:

1. Sieve flour, coco, baking powder and baking soda together.
2. Powder sugar in electric grinder.
3. Prepare a round mould.
4. Preheat oven to moderate heat.
5. Combine butter and sugar and beat till light and fluffy. Add eggs one by one and beat thoroughly.
6. Add flour mixture and milk alternately. Finally, add crushed peanuts and mix well. Pour in the mould.
7. Bake in the centre of the moderately hot oven for 40 to 45 minutes.
8. Remove and cool. Invert the cake on cooling rack for 30 minutes, remove from the pan.
9. Cut into the wedges before serving.

Serving: Serve it with warm cinnamon custard sauce.

6. Tender Hearts

(Traditional Sugar Cookies)

These old favourites are rich and tender. They are favourite of young and old alike and are excellent to be served anytime with beverages.

You Require: **Cooking Time:** 15 to 20 minutes for preparation and 10 to 12 minutes for baking.

Flour	1 and ½ cup	Baking powder	½ tsp
Baking soda	½ tsp	Salt	¼ tsp
Sugar	½ cup	Butter/shortening	½ cup
Milk	2 tbsp	Vanilla essence	1 tsp
Egg	1 no.		

Preparation and Cooking:

1. Preheat the oven to 180 degrees Celsius.
2. Combine and sieve flour, baking powder, baking soda and salt together.
3. Add sugar and sieve once again. If sugar is of big granules, coarsely grind it before mixing with flour mixture.
4. Cut in butter until the mixture resembles coarse meal. You may mix it with your fingertips lightly.
5. Blend in egg, milk and vanilla essence and mix once again.
6. Roll out on floured surface to 1/8th-inch thickness.
7. Cut with a 2 to 2 and ½-inch cutter. Take out as many cookies as possible. Reroll the remaining dough and use it up.
8. Place on ungreased baking tray and bake in moderately hot oven for 10 to 12 minutes.
9. Remove the tray and let the cookies cool. Remove with a palate knife and store in a clean dry jar.

Serving: Serve the cookies with tea or coffee.

Or serve them hot as a dessert with any dessert sauce.

Variation: Not in the basic recipe but in flavour. Reduce the quantity of vanilla to half and add ½ tsp cardamom powder or aniseeds to the mixture.

Tips: If you like, you can decorate the cookies with melted chocolate or melted jam or marmalade of your choice.

7. Roasted Berries

An easy-to-make delicious and elegant dessert; is prepared with a variety of berries available at a time. Here berries are just roasted to release their natural sweetness and are flavoured with castor sugar. This simple dish is not only delicious and colourful, but also a rich source of vitamins A and C.

You Require: **Cooking Time:** 15 minutes.

Fresh strawberries	400 gm	Black raisins	¼ cup
Pistachio nuts	¼ cup	Castor sugar	2 tbsp
Or (when in season)			
Strawberries	200 gm	Raspberries	200 gm
Blackberries	100 gm	Or blueberries	100 gm
Mint sprig	for garnishing	Or dry mint powder	1 tsp (opt)

Preparation and Cooking:

1. Rinse, dry and wipe the berries gently.

2. Warm the strawberries in heavy-based non-stick pan over medium heat, stirring regularly.
3. Add sugar and other ingredients of your combination, e.g., raisins and nuts or raspberries and blackberries etc and cook for 1 minute. Do not overcook and let berries be limp or lose shape.
4. Transfer to a serving dish.

Serving: Garnish with mint and serve immediately.

Tips: In the absence of blackberries and blueberries, add a hand full of black raisins, cleaned and soaked in warm water for 30 minutes.

8. Caramalized Bananas

A simple dish of bananas that is loved by the natives and others alike all over the world.

You Require: **Cooking Time:** 15 minutes.

Bananas	4 nos.	Sugar	½ cup
Rum/brandy	1 tbsp	Pistachio nuts	a few
Butter	1 tbsp leveled	Water	½ cup

Preparation and Cooking:

1. Heat butter and sugar together in a pan on high fire till the sugar is thoroughly melted and caramelized.
2. Lower the heat and add water. Simmer for a few seconds.
3. Meantime, peel the bananas and cut them into 4 slices each and put them in sugar syrup. Let them heat up on slow fire.
4. Chop pistachio nuts.
5. Add rum or brandy to the banana mixture.

Serving: Transfer the bananas with caramelized sugar to a serving dish and garnish with chopped pistachio nuts. Serve the dish warm.

Or serve bananas with vanilla ice cream and top it with 1 tbsp sugar syrup and nuts.

Tips: To avoid discolouration do not slice bananas in advance.

If you like, you may put 1 tbsp liquor in a spoon and ignite it, and then pour it over the dish just before serving.

Frozen Desserts

9. Exquisite Mango Sorbet

Exquisite 'fruit sorbets' are very popular through-out Mexico and different regions have developed their own variety of recipes according to the availability of seasonal and local fruits. Known as **nieves,** sorbets are traditional frozen desserts which are delicately flavoured with sugar and fresh fruit.

You Require: **Preparation Time:** 3 to 4 hours.

Mango pulp	3 cups	Lime-juice	1 tbsp
Or mangoes	4 to 6 nos.	Sugar	3 to 4 tbsp
Water	50 ml	Mango wedges for garnishing	
Or mint sprigs for garnishing			

Preparation:

1. Place mango pulp or peeled and chopped mangoes in a blender or food processor with sugar, water and lime juice and blend well till smooth.
2. Adjust sugar and lime juice according to the taste, if need be.
3. Freeze the mango mixture in an ice-cream maker or in a shallow container for 1 to 1 and ½ hour or until beginning to set (solidify).
4. Remove from the freezer and return to the blender; and blend to remove the ice crystals.
5. Return it to the freeze proof container and set it again to freeze for 3 to 4 hours.

Serving: Serve it in scoops or in pieces. Garnish the excellent sorbet with mango wedges or fresh mint sprigs and serve.

10. Chocolate Coffee Mousse

Coco/cacao is one of the most important Mexican contributions to the world. Chocolate is used in many forms as a beverage or to create cakes and various other dishes.

You Require: **Cooking Time:** 30 minutes and chilling time extra.

Condensed Milk (sweetened)	1 tin	Hot water of equal measure	1 tin
Or full cream milk	400 ml	Sugar	4 tbsp
Coco powder	3 tbsp	Or Cooking Chocolate	75 gm
Coffee powder	1 tbsp	Gelatin	4 tsp
Eggs	2 nos. large	Water to dissolve gelatin	¼ cup
Cream for garnishing	¼ to ½ cup (opt)		
Chocolate grated or chocolate chips for garnishing (opt)			
Pan of ice to fold soufflé on			

Preparation and Cooking:

1. Clean mould; smear it with a little cooking oil; rinse with water without touching inside; shake it and place in the deep freezer to chill.
2. Separate the egg yolks and whites.
3. Open the tin of condensed milk in a large bowl; mix hot water, coco powder, coffee powder and egg yolks. Beat thoroughly with rotary beater. Do not add sugar.

4. If you are not using condensed milk, then first make egg custard and then add coco and coffee to it. Cook it on slow fire of gas heat or in a microwave. In a micro-safe bowl, mix together egg yolks, sugar and milk; beat with a rotary beater/egg-beater and cook on HIGH for 2 minutes, stirring once. Now, cook egg custard on micro MEDIUM for 4 minutes, stirring every 2 minutes; take it out and mix coco or melted chocolate and coffee in it.
5. Mix gelatin with ¼ cup water and dissolve it on pan of hot water till clear and pour into the milk mixture. Beat it once again until well blended. Cool the mixture in the following manner.
6. Put enough water in a wide mouthed vessel or trove; place the mixture bowl in it to take out the heat; change water and add ice to the water; keep stirring the mixture to avoid any lumps. Mixture will start thickening.
7. Beat egg whites very stiff and fold into the thickening mixture.
8. Pour the mixture in the chilled mould and replace it in the deep freezer for 30 to 40 minutes or till set. Later cover with foil or cling film and place in the cold part of your refrigerator till used.

Note: Keep the covered souffle in the deep freezer only if it is going to be served next day or after a couple of days, but take it out at least 6 hours before use from the freezer and keep in the lower compartment of your refrigerator.

Serving: Loosen the soufflé with butter knife and unmould it in a chilled plate; cover it with cream and garnish with grated chocolate or chocolate sauce; and serve immediately.

Tips: Cold soufflés for desserts are generally served unmoulded, but you can set them in 6-small glass bowls too, and serve individually without un-moulding.

11. Raspberry Ice Cream

Raspberries are enjoyed in various ways in Mexico, and this ice cream is a noble example of the variety.

You Require: **Cooking Time:** 1 hour and freezing time extra.

Raspberries chopped	6 cups.	Sugar	2 cups
Lime	1 no.	Heavy cream	3 cups
Milk	1 and ½ cup	Egg yolks	6 nos.
Rose water	1 tbsp (opt)	White chocolate chopped	1 cup

Preparation and Cooking:

1. Combine raspberries, half the sugar and juice from the lime together in a micro safe bowl and cook on MEDIUM for 10 minutes, covered, stirring once in between. Stand it for 10 minutes and mash thoroughly with a wooden spoon, or pass through an electric blender.

2. Strain the pulp through a sieve into a bowl, pressing the berries to extract as much liquid as possible. Discard the seeds and cool the berry mixture.

   Note: You may cook berries on the top of gas stove also but stirring constantly.

3. Mix together heavy cream and milk in a saucepan and simmer gently.
4. Meanwhile, whisk egg yolks and remaining sugar together in a mixing bowl until pale yellow and fluffy.
5. Whisking constantly, pour the hot cream mixture, in a steady stream onto the egg yolks and blend thoroughly.
6. Transfer the custard to the saucepan and cook over low fire, stirring constantly with a wooden spoon, scraping the sides and the bottom of the pan till custard thickens to coat the back of the spoon.
7. Or place saucepan in a bigger pan filled half with hot water and cook custard over it. Pan with hot water will work like a double boiler and custard will not burn or stick to the bottom. Keep stirring till custard is thick enough to coat the back of the spoon.
8. Strain the custard in to a bowl and stir rose water. Cover the custard with a cling film or a cover to prevent formation of a film on the top and cool it at room temperature.
9. Mix the cooled raspberry mixture and custard together and chill thoroughly.
10. Here beat the mixture once with a rotary beater and set it for freezing. Add chopped chocolate and stir with a spatula.
11. Or 3 hours before serving, freeze the mixture in an ice cream maker according to the manufacturer's instructions till firm.

Serving: For the best results the ice cream should be frozen for 24 to 48 hours. Serve it chilled

Tips: Mexico has an old, deep rooted tradition of making frozen desserts. They are constantly creating the most tantalizing collection of frozen treats. From big cities to small towns and even on roadside eating joints, colourful ice creams, sorbets and raspados are sold everyday. The reason is that Mexico's mountainous geography and its latitude result in the perfect conditions for varied crops of fruits. Therefore several chains of ice cream around the country compete with each other to impress their consumers and guests with newer and exciting additions.

Raspados are made of shaved ice and it is flavoured with fruit syrups (like Indian ice Gola).

12. Watermelon Ice

One of the most popular ices prepared in Mexico is the watermelon ice. This preparation of ice is closer to granita that makes a flavourful, chile-spiced ice with coarse crystals that melt slowly on the tongue.

You Require: **Cooking Time:** 20 minutes and chilling time 3 to 4 hours.

Peeled and diced seeded watermelon 3 cups			
Freshly squeezed lemon juice 1 and ½ tbsp			
Or Lime Juice	¼ cup	Sugar	½ cup
Water	¼ cup	Pure chilli powder	a pinch
Lime/lemon wedges for garnishing (opt)			

Preparation and Cooking:

1. Mix sugar and water in a bowl and cook on medium heat until sugar is dissolved.
2. Or cook it in a microwave till sugar is dissolved. Cool to room temperature.
3. Combine the watermelon and sugar syrup in a blender and blend until smooth. Stop blender in between and scrape the sides down for smoothness. Pass the watermelon puree through a coarse sieve and pour into a shallow glass dish. Add chilli powder and lemon or lime juice and stir properly.
4. Place the dish on a flat surface in the deep freezer. When the edges of the ice start to freeze (after 30 to 40 minutes), stir the crystals from around the edges into the liquid in the centre.
5. Repeat the action each time the edges begin to freeze. Total freezing time will be between 3 to 4 hours. But it is important to stir the frozen parts into the still liquid part of the mixture to develop the proper coarse crystals.

Serving: Spoon the ice into small bowls or cocktail glasses; top with a lemon or lime wedge and serve immediately.

You may line the serving bowls or glasses with thin slices of mango or pineapple before putting the ice in them.

Tips: The ice can be prepared up to one day in advance, but not more than that.

13. Chocolate Sorbet

It is already mentioned above that one of the precious gifts of Mexico to the world is chocolate. In its simplest and ancient form, chocolate was a drink in which toasted, ground cacao beans were mixed with water, not milk, then foamed and served as an invigorating and restorative beverage reserved for nobles, clerics and governors etc. Mixing it with milk is the recent development. Interestingly, this creamy and chocolaty sorbet imparts the pleasant double flavour which comes from cocoa powder and chocolate.

You Require: **Cooking Time:** 20 t0 30 minutes and setting time extra.

Sugar	1 cup	Coco powder	½ cup
Water	2 cups	Bitter-sweet chocolate	200 gm
Salt	a pinch		

Preparation and Cooking:

1. Coarsely chop the chocolate and keep aside.
2. Combine sugar, coco and salt; mix with measured water and whisk.
3. Bring the liquid to the boiling point on medium heat, stirring constantly to dissolve sugar and coco.
4. Remove from the heat and cool it for 5 minutes or so; add the chocolate and stir until melted. Cool the sorbet mixture to the room temperature, cover and chill thoroughly.
5. At least 2 hours before serving, freeze the sorbet in an ice cream maker according to the manufacturer's instructions. Pack into a container with a tight fitting lid and freeze until firm
6. The sorbet can be kept in the freezer for up to 4 days. If the sorbet is frozen solid, let it stand at room temperature for 10 minutes before serving.

Serving: Serve single or double scoop individually in ice cream cups or small glass bowls.

Tips: if you do not have ice-cream maker, stir the coco-chocolate mixture placed in the deep freezer twice before it is set.

14. Caramel Custard

(Crème Caramel)

This caramelized sugar topped dish is one of Mexico's favourite desserts. In Mexican cuisine its origin cam be traced back to Spanish era. When eggs and milk were introduced, this and so many other puddings were innovated and later on became an integral part of Mexican traditional cuisine. This caramel flavoured, nice textured custard is one of the light puddings which one can make and enjoy anytime of the day.

You Require: **Cooking Time:** 1 hour 15 minutes and chilling time extra.

Condensed milk	1 tin of 400 gm	Eggs	3 nos. large
Egg yolk	1 no.	Milk	1 and ½ cup
Sugar	4 tbsp	Vanilla essence	1 tsp

Or if sweet condensed is not used then use the following ingredients:

Milk	3 cups	Eggs	3 nos.
Sugar	3 tbsp	Powder milk	3 tbsp
Vanilla essence	1 tsp	Sugar for caramelizing	4 tbsp

Preparation and Cooking:

1. Warm a soufflé mould or any other oven-proof dish in a preheated oven.
2. Put sugar in a heavy based pan over a low heat and let it melt slowly. Once melted boil quickly until it has caramelized. Pour into the soufflé mold or other dish and coat all over by carefully tipping the dish. Leave it to cool.

3. Beat the eggs and egg yolk in a separate bowl till creamy; add milk, condensed milk and vanilla essence and mix it thoroughly.
4. Pour into prepared (caramelized) dish; cover it with a piece of foil, but don't let the foil touch the custard.
5. Half fill a roasting tin with hot water and stand the dish with custard in it and steam-bake it in hot oven for 1 hour or till the custard is set.
6. Remove from the oven and cool it thoroughly. Cover and chill it under refrigeration for at least 2 hours. Invert it before serving.

Note: If you coat 6 small individual ovenproof bowls or ramekins with caramelized sugar and pour the pudding mixture in them, then steam bake for 25 to 30 minutes only. Rest, follow the same instructions.

Serving: Run a tip of a butter knife or a palate knife around the edge of the custard; place a serving dish on top and invert the custard mold. Let the caramel run over top and sides of the custard.

15. Fruits in Lemon Jelly

You Require: **Cooking Time:** 15 minutes. Chilling and setting time extra.

Mango	1 no.	Apple	1 no.
Pear	1 no.	Or Any other combination of soft and crisp fruits	1 no.
Lemon	1 no.		

For Jelly:

Water	2 and ½ cups	Fresh lemon-juice	¼ cup
Gelatin	4 tsp	Sugar	¼ cup or to taste
Yellow food colour	2 drops (opt)		

Or

One packet light-colour flavoured jelly crystals of your choice, for example, lemon, pineapple or cranberry can be used.

Preparation and Cooking:

1. Take a shallow glass dish; rinse and chill in the deep freezer.
2. Boil sugar and water together; dissolve gelatin in 3 tbsp water and add to sugared water; boil till all gelatin crystals are clear and then add fresh lemon juice. Or dissolve jelly crystals of your choice according to the instructions on the packet.
3. Remove from fire and cool under refrigeration.
4. Peel mango and cut in any desired shape. Cut apple and pear, too, in the same shape. You may peel apple.

5. Remove the chilled dish from deep freezer; pour half of the lemon jelly in it; arrange the cut fruits carefully over it, and gently pour the remaining jelly on top.
6. Place the dish in the deep freezer for 30 minutes; remove, cover with cling film and keep in the coldest part of the refrigerator till in use.

Serving: Serve it after a spicy Mexican meal at lunch or dinner.

16. Chilli-flavoured Chocolate Cake

You Require: **Cooking Time:** 40 minutes.

Bitter-sweet chocolate	10 ounce	Unsalted butter	200 gm
Sugar	¾ cup	Eggs	3 nos.
Pureed red chilli	1 tbsp	Orange juice	¼ cup
Flour	½ cup	Sugar for coating the moulds	¼ cup
A pinch	of salt	Small moulds	
Cinnamon custard sauce	to serve with	Or A baking tray	6 nos.

Preparation and Cooking:

1. Butter the moulds and sprinkle sugar to coat evenly.
2. Place a kettle full of water on fire. Preheat the oven.
3. Put chocolate in a heat-proof bowl. Combine sugar and orange juice in a separate bowl and cook on medium heat stirring all the time till the sugar is melted.
4. Pour the sugar syrup over the chocolate and whisk gently until the chocolate is melted. Add butter and blend.
5. Beat in the eggs one by one. Whisk in the chilli paste; stir in the flour and mix.
6. Divide the batter equally in the prepared moulds and place them in a baking tray.
7. Pour enough hot water into the baking tray to come half way up the sides of moulds.
8. Bake in a moderately hot oven for 30 to 35 minutes. Cool slightly.

Serving: Unmould the cakes onto the serving individual plates and decorate with cinnamon custard sauce.

Serve hot or at room temperature.

17. Cinnamon Custard Sauce

You Require: **Cooking Times:** 30 minutes

Heavy cream	2 cups	Eggs	2 no. large
Sugar	½ cup	Cinnamon stick	2 pieces of 2 inches each
Lime zest	3 pieces of 1 inch each		

Note: Lime zest can be removed with a vegetable peeler from a fresh lime.

Preparation and Cooking

1. In a small heavy pan, combine cream, cinnamon and zest together and just boil over medium fire/heat.
2. Remove from the heat.
3. Beat eggs and sugar together in a mixing bowl till well blended. Whisking constantly, add hot cream slowly to the egg mixture.
4. Place the sauce-pan over medium heat and stir continuously with a wooden spoon until thick and custard starts coating the back of the spoon.
5. Remove from fire and strain the sauce through a fine sieve into a bowl.
6. Cover the sauce with cling wrap or a piece of aluminium foil and cool at room temperature.
7. Chill the sauce under refrigeration at least for 2 hours before serving.

Serving: Serve the **Cinnamon custard** sauce with cakes, cookies or over fresh cut fruits as a dessert.

Or eat it all by itself for dessert.

Tips: The sauce can be prepared 2 days in advance and stored in the cool part of a refrigerator.

Fruits in Lemon Jelly